BUYING,

AND MOV

David Lewis is one of the country's most experienced personal financial writers. He is author of several books on investment, pensions and insurance, including *The Savers and Investors Guide*, which is published annually by Wisebuy Publications and has sold over a quarter of a million copies. From 1976 to 1986 he was editor of the *Daily Mail*'s *Money Mail*, having previously been editor of the monthly magazine *Money Management*, and before that worked as a financial researcher on *Which?* magazine. David Lewis is now an independent writer and editor.

TEACH YOURSELF BOOKS

What the press has said about this book:

'One of the best books ever written for would-be homebuyers.'
Daily Telegraph

'Young people planning to buy their own home will find some worthwhile reading.' *Sunday Times*

'. . . covers most aspects of the home owning process in a clear manner which will be helpful to the layperson.'
Law Society Gazette

'Throughout the book there are useful hints on how to save money and how to calculate possibly unseen costs.'
National Council of Citizens' Advice Bureaux Book List

'David Lewis gives detailed explanations and practical advice on all aspects of home ownership.' *The Bankers' Magazine*

'Housebuyers looking for expert guidance can invest in a useful new Teach Yourself Book . . . David Lewis offers down to earth advice on how to search for the best value, the size of the mortgage you can expect and finds out the hidden extra costs.'
News of the World

'A useful new book.' *The Guardian*

'. . . invaluable in explaining and advising on house purchase or selling, gazumping, conveyancing and how to look for the best bargain.' *Glasgow Herald*

'This is the sort of book that could save you many times over what you spend on it; not to mention the savings it will help you make in emotional worry.' *Huddersfield Daily Examiner*

BUYING, SELLING AND MOVING HOME

David Lewis

TEACH YOURSELF BOOKS
Hodder and Stoughton

First published 1980 as
Buying and Selling Your Home
Second edition 1984
Third edition 1986
Fourth edition 1988

British Library Cataloguing in Publication Data
Lewis, David B. (David Benjamin), *1946–*
Buying, selling and moving home.—4th ed.
(Teach yourself books)
1. Great Britain. Residences. Purchase –
Manuals
I. Title
333.33′8′0941

ISBN 0 340 49402 6

Printed in Great Britain for
Hodder and Stoughton Educational,
a division of Hodder and Stoughton Ltd,
Mill Road, Dunton Green, Sevenoaks, Kent,
by Richard Clay Ltd, Bungay, Suffolk
Photoset by Rowland Phototypesetting Ltd,
Bury St Edmunds, Suffolk

Contents

Acknowledgments

My thanks to those who read the draft of the first edition of this book, and also this revised edition. They include three English solicitors and one Scottish: all of them made many helpful suggestions and to my surprise and delight actually liked the contents.

Also my thanks to the organisations which supplied information and the permission to reproduce tabular material, the source of which is given with each table.

Last but not least, my thanks to Susan Lewis who helped with the research, thoroughly edited my drafts and made innumerable helpful suggestions.

Preface

This book is for first time buyers and sellers: for people who are in the process of buying a house or flat for the first time, who are thinking of doing so in the future, or who already own their first home but have not yet experienced selling a home as well as buying one at the same time.

Whilst every effort has been made to ensure that the information in this book was correct at the time it went to press, neither the author nor the publishers can accept liability for any errors or omissions, nor can they accept responsibility with regard to the standing of any organisations mentioned in the text. The list of names and addresses in Appendix 3 should enable you to get a second opinion on any point which is particularly important to you, or which may have changed.

If readers have any experiences which might be of interest to me regarding future editions, I would be happy to hear from them; write to me care of the publishers. However I am unable to give personal advice.

David Lewis

1

Why Own a Home?

An Englishman's home is his castle – or so the saying goes. And what better way of ensuring the security of that castle than by owning it. Every year a higher and higher proportion of houses and flats become owner-occupied, either bought outright, or with the help of a mortgage. And each year nearly 600,000 homes are bought by first time buyers.

Some 64% of the twenty-one million homes in Britain are owner-occupied; the rest of the population live mainly in rented accommodation, either from local authorities and new town corporations (26%) or from private owners (6%). Other sources such as homes tied to a job (2%) and housing associations (2%) account for a very small proportion.[1]

So if you want to buy your own home you are in good company. Nearly 80% of the respondents to a survey[2] gave owner-occupation as their ideal in two years' time, while only 61% were already owner-occupiers. The survey showed that the desire to become an owner-occupier was strong among tenants: nearly one in two respondents who currently rented ideally wanted to become owner-occupiers within two years.

The proportion of home ownership is similar abroad. In the Common Market countries during the early 1980s, 49% of homes were owned by the occupier, with the highest proportion in Ireland (76%) and the lowest in West Germany (44%), and France (50%) and Italy (56%) coming in between. In Australia and New Zealand, 70% of homes were owner-occupied, whereas in the USA the figure was 65%.[2,3]

These high figures are hardly surprising. Owning your own home has many obvious advantages over renting, even assuming you can find somewhere to rent. One of the intangible reasons is that you feel you have freedom to do as you want. You are independent. And people seem to be happier with their lot when they own rather than rent. You can choose where to live, and usually when and how to decorate.

On the other hand, the cost of repairs and maintenance, and the necessity to organise these yourself, is one of the few disadvantages of owner-occupation. Another is the heavy financial burden which people have to take on when they buy a home for the first time. Mortgage arrears, after rent arrears, are the most common reason for homelessness, and have risen significantly during the 1980s.

As an investment

The most important reason for owning your home is that you are making an investment which, in terms of value for money, most people will find impossible to repeat. Owning a home is such a good investment because house prices often exceed the rate of inflation in the economy as a whole. In April 1988, house price inflation was 25%, while inflation in general was 3.9% over the previous 12 months. This does not mean that house price rises will always exceed inflation – or that you can never lose money by owning your home. But if the past is any guide to the future, inflation is likely to continue and house prices on average are likely to go up by at least as much. Owner-occupied homes are also exempt from capital gains tax when you dispose of them (for exceptions see Chapter 12).

You might wonder why rises in house prices are such an advantage. After all, if you do not own one already, the rise in prices may appear sickening. But once you own your home, and live in it for a few years, you will soon see how price rises can work to your advantage. Table 1 shows the average price of homes bought by first time buyers through building societies since 1977, together with their average mortgage and average income. Take the average couple who bought in 1977. Suppose their mortgage was exactly the average at that time – £8,515. The mortgage interest rate was then 9.5%, so their monthly payments came to £53.15 after basic rate income tax relief at 35%. In 1987 many building societies charged a

Table 1 First time buyers

Year	*Average price* £	*Average mortgage* £	*Average income* £
1977	10,857	8,515	4,800
1978	12,023	9,602	5,283
1979	14,918	11,286	6,290
1980	17,533	12,946	7,749
1981	18,166	14,361	8,248
1982	17,762	15,109	8,602
1983	19,513	16,611	8,899
1984	22,174	18,786	9,754
1985	23,742	20,260	10,466
1986	27,444	23,640	11,669
1987	30,097	25,485	12,444

Source: The Building Societies Association. (In 1982 there was an exceptional fall in the price of homes bought by first time buyers.)

mortgage interest rate of around 10%, which meant their payments had risen to £58.29 a month, again after basic rate tax relief at 27%.

However, average incomes increased by much more over the same period, as you can see from Table 1: their income could easily have risen from £4,800 to £12,444. With promotion at work their income could have risen by much more. If the same couple had been first time buyers of the same house at the end of 1987, they would have had to find the payments on the then average mortgage of £25,485 (£174.46 a month in late 1987) out of their earnings of £12,444 a year. Alternatively, they would have had to provide a much larger deposit than was needed only ten years earlier.

Changing home

Of course most people do not stay in the same home all their lives. In a survey of borrowers with recent mortgages from the Nationwide Building Society,[4] the results show that the average stay in the former home was under five years, with 10% of previous owner-occupiers having spent only a year in their home. In an earlier survey by the Alliance Building Society,[5] it was found that the longest stay in a current house was sixty-six years. But 20% said they expected to move house within two years, and another 20% in two to five years' time. However, some people expect to stay put for a long time. 27% expected to stay in their present homes indefinitely – and another 5% for ever.

Why do people move home? The surveys cast light on this too. As well as financial reasons and job considerations, common reasons were the desire for more space, a better location, more privacy or a larger garden.

Apart from those who simply wanted to buy a home of their own (first time buyers), other less common reasons were to escape some environmental nuisance, or were related to marriage or children's schooling. A tiny proportion moved house in order to accommodate an elderly relative, or because they wanted less space in the home or a smaller garden.

So you are unlikely to be content for long to sit back in your castle and reflect on how lucky you are to have such a small mortgage now in relation to what today's first time buyers are having to cope with. You will go in search of a better home, for whatever reason, and probably not far from where you already live – most people move less than ten miles from where they were before, and according to the Nationwide Building Society survey, 60% move less than five miles. You will not be able to get a larger mortgage than a first time buyer if he earns the same as you. But what you will have is the increased value of your present house to invest in the new one.

Table 2 show the same kind of information as Table 1, but this

Table 2 Former owner-occupiers

Year	*Average price* £	*Average mortgage* £	*Average income* £
1977	16,246	9,101	5,558
1978	18,792	10,611	6,161
1979	24,074	11,837	7,101
1980	28,959	13,359	8,688
1981	30,110	15,384	9,419
1982	30,634	17,316	10,178
1983	34,260	19,672	10,969
1984	36,717	21,483	11,703
1985	39,390	23,300	12,702
1986	45,200	27,146	14,165
1987	49,987	29,487	15,044

Source: The Building Societies Association.

time it refers to former owner-occupiers; that is, people who already own their home, and who are buying a new one with a mortgage. You can be fairly sure that in most cases these people are increasing their mortgage when they move.

The table shows that whilst former owner-occupiers obtain slightly higher advances, on account of their slightly higher incomes, the value of the homes they are buying is much greater than the value of those bought by first time buyers. While they are paying much the same for their mortgages, their earlier home ownership allows them to enjoy larger and more luxurious homes at little extra cost because of the substantial deposits they are able to provide.

The costs of buying versus renting

The greatest difference between buying and renting is that when you buy you have to find a large lump sum of money at the outset. A mortgage is a means by which you can pay off that lump sum by instalments over many years – but despite the increased availability of 100% mortgages, it is still rare that you will get a mortgage for 100% of the purchase price. The exceptions, where it is quite common, are when you are a tenant buying at a discount the house or flat you already live in, or where the mortgage is provided by a local authority. Even with a large mortgage you need a lump sum, if not for the deposit then to cover the cost of legal expenses, possible repairs and decorations, and new fixtures and fittings, expenses which, if you rent, often do not apply, or may be provided by the landlord (see Chapter 4 on the costs of buying).

However, private landlords often charge one month's rent in advance, and may require a deposit in advance of another month's rent – and there may be a flat agency charge to pay as well. You may also be expected to pay for 'fixtures and fittings'. The cost of these fixtures and fittings is often inflated, in spite of the fact that it is usually against the law for a landlord to grant, or a tenant to transfer, a residential tenancy in exchange for extra money. None of these costs normally apply to Council tenancies.

Comparing averages can be misleading. According to a Government report[6]: 'There is no incontrovertible way of making the comparison [on subsidies] between home owners and local authority tenants to show the extent of the advantage of one group over the other or even to show which group "does better".'

With privately owned housing, the subsidy (tax relief) is more concentrated – it is given to those with the largest mortgages (up to £30,000) who pay the largest amount of interest. Contrary to popular belief, these are not necessarily the rich, but are more likely to be first time buyers who have little capital of their own to put up. Council tenants pay the same rent as their neighbours however long they have been tenants – although housing benefit (previously called rent rebates) and rent allowances for private tenants can lower the cost for the less well off. Nowadays many first time buyers are couples who have spent a short time in rented accommodation, or living with parents or in-laws, or who seek to buy their first home before they get married. The message of the statistics is quite clear: the sooner you get on the home ownership ladder, at however modest a level, the more likely you are eventually to own the house of your dreams.

Notes

1 *General Household Survey 1983; Housing and Construction Statistics*, 1984. Updated to 1987.
2 *Housing Tenure*, The Building Societies Association, June 1983.
3 Nationwide Building Society Bulletins: *Housing and the European Community*, 1979; *World Housing*, October 1980.
4 Nationwide Building Society, *Home Buyers Moving Survey*, September 1982.
5 *Housing Research Unit*, University of Surrey, 1977. Similar results were found by the *General Household Survey 1977*, HMSO, 1979.
6 *Housing Policy Technical Review*, Chapter 5, HMSO, 1977.

2

Finding Somewhere to Buy

Most people who advise on house purchase start by asking how much you can afford and then proceed to see what kind of house or flat suits your pocket rather than your needs. I think you should first try and sort out in your mind what kind of home would suit you best, and if after a long search you cannot afford it, then you can settle for the nearest which you can afford, sacrificing some features which you rate as less important. On average, it takes ten months from starting your search to moving in. You are likely to view about ten houses inside and twenty-seven outside.[1]

Where to buy?

The main criterion for choosing a house or flat is that it should be a sensible distance from your place of work. If you and your partner both work – and your jobs are in different directions – your scope for choice of location is going to be limited to somewhere between the two jobs or else one of you is likely to end up changing your job before long.

If you work in central London you might choose to commute quite long distances by rail; but remember rail services do vary, and a sixty mile journey which might only take an hour on one route could take two and a half on a less popular line. Check the cost of a season ticket to your place of work, and whether your employer would give you an interest-free season ticket loan. In other locations you are more likely to travel by bus, so check on the service's frequency and convenience.

Most people also like to live near relatives and people they know.

If this is important to you, you will have considerably restricted the area of your search. In a city, for instance, you often find people divide into north of the river and south of the river people. Rarely do they think of crossing to the other side in search of a home; they prefer to stick to the area they know.

Other points about the general location of your new home will assume different levels of importance depending on your circumstances. For instance, if you have children of school age, the availability and quality of local schools and their distance from your home will be of prime consideration. In fact some people move home in order to get their children into the catchment area of good state schools. If you do this you should make quite sure that your children will get into the school of your choice – and that your new home is in the catchment area. I have never heard of such a case, but I presume that catchment areas can change – and it would be unfortunate if someone moved house in search of better education for their children only to find they are not much better off than they were before.

Local transport, as opposed to commuting, is also worth thinking about, especially in rural areas where public transport can sometimes be very sparse. If you cannot get to the railway station without a car, then your partner is either going to be an unpaid chauffeur twice daily or you will need a second car; according to figures put out regularly by the AA, the cost of running a car seems to run a close second to the cost of owning a home. A decision to run two cars should not be taken lightly. Perhaps this is the time to ask for a company car?

Availability of shops is also important. In the country, if you have a car, it is easy to drive to the nearest village or town. But the larger the town, the greater becomes the proliferation of yellow lines, parking restrictions and traffic jams and it is often more convenient to walk to the shops. So, unless the nearest shop is less than a quarter of an hour's walk away, you are likely to want to take the car or a convenient bus.

Whether to live in the town or in the country is a decision which seems to perplex some people. I live in a town and I know people who live in the country; we seem to be equally happy. But that may be because I live in an area of town where there is a lot of open space. Parks and trees and squares add to the quality of life and you can be sure that such amenities will be reflected in the price of the home you are seeking.

House prices

A host of factors influence the price of a house. The most obvious effect of this is the range of prices you can pay for identical houses situated in different parts of the country. Not only do the prices for similar houses vary nationally but they rise and (less commonly) fall at different rates.

The most costly homes are to be found in the outer London suburbs. In Inner London, the prices of homes vary widely according to location, just like the game of Monopoly, with Mayfair and Park Lane still the most costly and the Old Kent Road still amongst the cheapest. The next most expensive area is the rest of the South East, which, broadly speaking, is the area bordering London within commuter range.

The price of homes thus reflects the availability of work and the convenience of transport to work. Equally attractive villages in Sussex and Hampshire, more or less the same distance from London, will have significantly different house prices if one has easy

Table 3 Index of average house prices: by region and type

	Detached	*Semi-detached*	*Terraced*	*Flats*
United Kingdom	100	100	100	100
Greater London	212	208	192	132
South East	154	152	137	98
South West	108	111	103	79
East Anglia	101	111	100	75
East Midlands	76	71	63	54
West Midlands	82	77	65	51
Yorkshire & Humberside	69	64	51	45
North West	78	71	55	54
Northern	71	67	54	39
Wales	70	66	57	53
Scotland	70	79	77	56
N. Ireland	64	61	46	—

Source: Halifax Building Society: House prices in last quarter 1987. Index calculated from prices in the survey.

access by rail or motorway to London, and another has not. If you are looking for a retirement home, the best bargains are, by contrast, found in the more isolated rural areas of the country.

When to buy?

There is a popular season for house buying and selling. It starts in January, but most activity seems to take place in the spring, with April and May as the peak months. I suspect the actual amount of buying and selling activity depends a great deal on the local weather. With a particularly mild winter, it probably begins earlier; with a sharp cold spell with snow at the end of March, people probably put it off for a while. It can be quite depressing tramping around from one expensive unsuitable house to another – and if it is pouring with rain or you are chilled by a bitter wind, you are more than likely to want to give up and go to the cinema instead.

On the other hand, for a buyer, if you can bear it, bad weather is just the right time to be house hunting. It will show the house at its worst – and if you like it then, you will certainly love it when the sun is shining. What is more, particularly if prices are rising, other house hunters are likely to be after the same property as you are. But you will be on the spot – while your possible competitors are at the cinema. You must hope that the seller thinks nobody else is interested – not that they have merely been put off by the bad weather.

A shorter season occurs in September. There is not much activity in July or August, when most people go on holiday, nor in November or December presumably because it gets dark very early and people are immersed in Christmas festivities. But if you happen to be looking at such times, you are more likely to pick up a bargain. People selling in November or July, for example, usually have some special reason to do so, rather than wait for the traditional seasons. They may be moving home to take up a new job in another part of the country, or a previous offer may have fallen through for reasons entirely unconnected with the house. They may be getting divorced or want the money urgently. Or they may just have been asking too much during the season and nobody made them an offer. Do not hesitate to ask why someone is intending to move, especially if you think there is some reason connected with the house – perhaps they hated every minute they spent in it! Most likely their answer will be much more down to earth.

What type of house or flat?

What type of house you buy is usually determined by what you can afford and the space you need. Most people look for something which has a minimum of a sitting room, kitchen, bathroom, and indoor wc, and two bedrooms – one for themselves, and one for guests or children. In addition, many people will probably want three or four bedrooms in total, a dining or second reception room, a downstairs toilet, and possibly a study or breakfast room. These seemingly basic requirements can disguise enormous variations in size. It is therefore unwise to set your own particular needs too rigidly. Remember, some three bedroom houses can be larger than four bedroom ones – and you should think hard as to how much you will actually use that tiny guest room. Perhaps a larger bedroom for each of the children might be more useful.

Homes come in all shapes and sizes; they are usually classified as terraced; semi-detached; detached; purpose-built flat or maisonette; converted flat or maisonette; and bungalow. The availability of each type of accommodation varies between different parts of the country. Table 4 shows where different types of property are likely to be found. Flats are more likely to be found in Greater London and Scotland – terraced houses in the North and Midlands.

Terraced houses

Terraced houses are currently the most popular type of house for first time buyers. Most are in towns and they tend to be relatively cheap compared with other houses. They also can be very small: a typical terrace may originally have had 'two up and two down'. Nowadays you can expect to buy them with an added back extension comprising a kitchen and bathroom. Sometimes the rooms upstairs have been reorganised to make three tiny bedrooms – or the two reception rooms knocked into one to create more space.

The main drawback to a terraced house is the lack of space – if a couple start having children they soon grow out of their terraced home; until then they are likely to be very happy with it. According

Table 4 Regional variation of types of houses

	Dwellings as % of total in each region				
	Detached	*Semi-detached*	*Terraced*	*Purpose-built flat*	*Converted flat and others*
Great Britain	16	33	28	15	8
Greater London	6	20	25	26	23
South East	24	33	25	10	8
South West	22	34	25	9	10
East Anglia	30	36	22	7	5
East Midlands	24	40	26	6	4
West Midlands	12	41	30	12	5
Yorks & Humberside	14	42	31	8	5
North West	9	37	36	11	6
Northern	8	42	35	11	4
Wales	19	35	34	5	7
Scotland	13	18	20	40	9

Source: The General Household Survey 1976, HMSO 1978.

to the Alliance Building Society[1] the highest failure rate in obtaining mortgages on the type of house of the purchaser's choice included those looking for terraced houses and those wanting wings of large houses; this may have been caused by a certain resistance in the past to old property amongst building societies and the fact that terraced houses usually predominate in inner city areas where societies used not to lend. But the high proportion of first time buyers who do buy terraced houses with a building society mortgage shows their popularity.

Semi-detached houses

Semi-detached conjures up a vision of suburbia; and a great many semi-detached houses will turn out to be very similar in appearance, style and size. They were mostly built between 1919 and 1939, and were sold then for as little as £500 each. The typical layout is kitchen, sitting room and dining room downstairs; two reasonably sized and one tiny bedroom, with a bathroom and separate wc, upstairs. There are also larger, four bedroomed versions which have a breakfast room, and some may have a downstairs toilet. Semis built more recently are likely to be similar in layout. However, those built during the period 1945 to 1959 may be less attractive than older ones, often having smaller dimensions and a different finish – plain red brick compared with the attractive pebble-dash popular in the thirties. Few people set out to live in a 'semi'. A great many end up in one.

Semis are the most popular choice for people 'trading up'; that is, moving from their first owned home to a larger one. The move may either be from a smaller semi, or from a terraced house or a flat.

Detached houses

The main virtue of a detached house is that it *is* detached. You can usually walk all the way round it. You do not share any walls with neighbours so you will not be disturbed by noise coming through the walls; nor will you cause such a disturbance yourself. Detached houses tend to be larger than other types of houses with the same number of rooms. They are also likely to have larger gardens. Other factors such as age, design and size are also likely to be important to you, but unfortunately, if you are a first time buyer you are unlikely to be able to afford one.

Purpose-built flats

Purpose-built flats are blocks of flats which were originally built as flats. They are mostly on long leases (except in Scotland) and you pay a small ground rent – say £50 a year; you also have to pay your share of the cost of maintenance and services (e.g. porter, lifts, outside decorations and repairs) and the charges of the managing agents who keep the place running. These charges rise annually as costs rise. Older people who do not want to be bothered with the responsibilities of organising maintenance themselves often prefer purpose-built flats. Generally a residents' association is formed and there is nearly always someone willing to take up issues with the managing agents on behalf of all the tenants. Similar considerations apply to the so-called 'mansion' or refurbished blocks of flats. The only difference is that the cost of maintenance is likely to be higher when expensive items like roofs, lifts and communal heating need to be repaired or replaced.

A few blocks of flats are owned by landlords who can make even an owner-tenant's life a misery. It is worth asking what the landlord is like (a neighbour might tell you more frankly) and whether there have been any serious disputes over service charges.

Residents' associations are not without their problems. Often they tend to be organised by one or two 'public spirited' individuals who, as a result of the apathy of the other residents, may represent their own taste or views as that of all the residents to the landlord. The result may be changes made in your name of which you do not approve.

Converted flats

Converted flats are mainly found in London although they do exist elsewhere. They are often large Victorian family houses which are big enough to contain a good sized two bedroom flat on each of three floors and a basement; some houses are large enough to contain two small flats or one large one on each floor. Sometimes an extra flat is added in the roof space. The obligations with a converted flat are similar to a purpose-built one. They are popular with first time buyers, some of whom may have previously been private tenants in the same flat.

A converted flat no longer presents any difficulty when it comes to raising a mortgage, provided it is self-contained. The main difference between a converted flat and a purpose-built one is that the landlord, who only gets a small ground rent, is not likely to be interested in acting as unpaid managing agent. And, there being so few tenants, they need a unanimous decision before they can put pressure on the landlord. There can also be problems when the landlord lives in the block – or where he or she is elderly, or some of the other residents are elderly, and you are young.

A typical complaint is that the landlord does not clean the common staircase adequately. Often it is better for the tenants to agree to arrange this sort of thing themselves, rather than pay for services arranged by the landlord or agent with which they are not satisfied. These converted flats often have gardens – sometimes the use is shared by all the flats, sometimes it is exclusive to the resident of the basement or 'garden' flat – and sometimes it is even cordoned off into a zone for each resident. If you want a garden to yourself, make quite sure that you really have it. I know of a case where someone bought a garden flat thinking he had sole use of the garden; he entirely replanted it at his own expense only to find the other residents turning up with their deckchairs on the first hot summer day, and they had every right to do so.

Some converted flats do not have a separate water supply. This will only cause difficulties if the residents of one flat turn off the water when they go away on holiday, depriving the other flats in the block of their water supply.

Maisonettes and Bungalows

Maisonettes are like mini-blocks of flats. They often look like semi-detached or terraced houses – but there is a separate dwelling upstairs and downstairs. Sometimes the term maisonette is used to describe a flat occupying two floors. However, the main difference from a flat is that you have your own front door on to the street.

Bungalows are in demand from elderly people and the disabled. The reason is obvious; they do not want to climb stairs, but like to retain their own garden. However, they are not very common.

Old, modern or brand new?

Whether you want an old or modern house is purely a matter of taste. First time buyers often apparently prefer modern houses. So long as the house has been well maintained, there will be little difference between the prices of older and more modern houses which offer the same accommodation and facilities. The standard of houses built recently is said to be a considerable improvement on that of those built fifteen years ago. Unfortunately you are likely to get considerably less for your money in terms of size and number of rooms, and perhaps also size of garden.

You can of course buy a plot of land and get a builder to build the house of your dreams to your own design. Around 8,000 people do this every year. However, most new houses are speculatively built by those whose business is building houses for sale.

With a new house you can buy from the plan – that is, put down a deposit to reserve your house even before it is built. You can expect the price to rise between the time you do this and the time you complete the transaction. You would be wise to inspect a show house – that is, a similar house to your own which is finished and put on show – before you commit yourself. Rooms can look deceptively large on a plan. Remember also that builders invariably choose the best house or flat as a show house – and others on the same estate may be less attractively situated.

New houses have the disadvantage of having to be run-in.[4] The garden is often not made up – and you may have to buy top soil to cover rubble left behind after the building. You will almost certainly have trouble with condensation – a typical newly built house contains 1,500 gallons of water which have to be dried out.[3] There can be other teething problems, too, such as delays in the completion of the house – one person told me of having to move in before the tiles had been laid on the kitchen floor. According to a survey in July 1984 by *Which?* magazine, owners would be more likely to buy again from three national building firms: Bovis, Bryant and Wates.

National House-Building Council

There are often minor, and sometimes major, defects to be put right on new houses. The National House-Building Council, with which all the large firms of developers and builders and many smaller ones are registered, offers an important protection to purchasers of new houses.[4] The Council has laid down minimum standards of workmanship, material and design – and the Council is supposed to ensure that during the first two years from purchase, the builder puts right at his own expense any defect resulting from his failure to comply with these standards. However, you must complain to the builder in writing within the time limit.

In the third to tenth years the protection is limited to major structural defects not covered elsewhere. The worth of this cover was brought home to some residents on an estate near Colchester where a large number of houses started to collapse as a result of having been built on a former rubbish dump. You are safeguarded against inflation up to 12% a year, but there is a maximum of £160,000 even if your house cost more than this. A building society may not lend on a house less than ten years old unless it has an NHBC certificate. There is a separate scheme for six years' protection on newly converted flats and houses with a maximum of £50,000.

Freehold or leasehold?

With a freehold you have no landlord, you pay no ground rent, usually you are beholden to no one else – and you own the house for ever. With a leasehold you have a landlord to whom you must pay ground rent for a certain number of years until the lease runs out. Most leases run for ninety-nine years; as the lease runs out, the value of your home starts to decline. However, under the Leasehold Reform Act 1967 you often have the right to buy the freehold or get a fifty year extension to the lease of your house (but not of a flat).[5] The differences can become blurred because you may have to pay a rent charge or chief rent on freehold property in some parts of England[6] or *feu duty* in Scotland.[7]

Houses or flats with leases granted for twenty-one years or less have no rights to have their leases extended unless the lease contains an option to do so. You are unlikely to get anyone to lend you money on such short leases as by the time you have repaid them the lease will be nearly expired, and your asset will no longer be a worthwhile security.

Covenants

Leases usually contain a number of covenants which bar the resident from doing such things as letting any part of the premises (except, perhaps, the garage), using the premises for business purposes, displaying any sign (including a For Sale notice), erecting any building or structure, changing the fences, keeping pets, singing or playing a musical instrument or stereo system after 11 pm, or even putting up a television aerial.

However, freehold houses can also have covenants (called 'restrictive covenants') just like those listed above – and on housing estates these have been known to include forbidding the running of a mobile fish and chip shop from the home, or car breaking in the garden! More irritating are those preventing your changing the colour of your front door without permission of a residents' association, or determining that you should hang net curtains in the windows.

Often the restrictions are ignored, especially if the person who might want to enforce them (like the ground landlord of a lease) is not around. But with freeholds there is no landlord, so policing of the covenants is only significant on housing estates where it is often in the hands of the residents' association – possibly run by neighbours who care rather strongly if you move in and start painting the front door red, when it has always been white.

Mobile homes, caravans and houseboats

Caravans, often referred to as mobile homes, have one great disadvantage. Most people who own them do not own the 'pitch' on which they stand. Under the Mobile Homes Act 1983, they have the right, with a few exceptions, to get a written agreement giving security indefinitely.

Some mobile homes are more akin to 'prefabs' than caravans. The distinguishing feature from ordinary homes is that they are not attached to the ground – generally they are placed on a concrete bed on the site. Also, as they are not intended to be moved, they cannot easily be towed away to another site if the rent for the site increases beyond that which the tenant can afford. When you sell your mobile home, you have to pay 10% commission to the site owner.

By their very method of construction, even the highest quality mobile homes have a much shorter life than conventional housing – seldom more than twenty to thirty years – while a conventional house might last one hundred or more. They tend to be small, and the materials used may make them a fire hazard. As a deteriorating asset, they cannot be bought with a mortgage, although the purchaser may be able to obtain credit from a bank or finance company. Maintenance, however, is less costly and complex than with a conventional home, which may make them attractive to elderly people. There is an official leaflet setting out the rights of mobile home owners.[8]

Houseboats

Houseboats are a similar case to mobile homes. Unless you own the mooring you will have to sail off somewhere else if the rent gets to be more than you can afford. Like some mobile homes, many houseboats are not designed to be moved easily, so this may involve you in some expense. Unlike mobile homes, they are also likely to need quite a lot of maintenance – painting more regularly than a house and making sure that no leaks spring up. I have known only one person who lived on a houseboat. She went out one night to the pub with her husband – and they returned to find their home had sunk!

What to look for

By now you may be itching to get started in your search for your new home. Finding out about available property is fairly straightforward. Get in touch with all the estate agents in the area where you want to live. Tell them the sort of thing you want and ask them to send you details of anything suitable which they get in. In Scotland most property is sold through Solicitors' Property Centres.[9]

It is worth calling in at an estate agent's office – if only because you are more likely to get better service that way. The fact that you take the trouble to call shows him you are serious. If a bank or building society has indicated its willingness to lend to you, make sure the agent knows. If you already have finance fixed up, you are a much better prospect to him. If you are moving to an area a long way from where you live at present, make use of the Homelink service of the National Association of Estate Agents, or a national firm of estate agents which can either provide you with information on the area you have chosen, or put you in touch with a local estate agent.

Do not just rely on agents sending you information, but drive or walk round the area looking for 'For Sale' boards. Some may be 'under offer', but it is often worth a telephone call to find out. Also look for advertisements in local and national newspapers. This is where people advertise who are selling without an agent. It is also worth asking any local people you know whether neighbours are thinking of moving. Even a short visit to the local pub might be more rewarding than you think.

There are a number of weekly magazines which specialise in house advertisements, like *Dalton's Weekly* and the *London Weekly Advertiser*. There are also monthly magazines with names like *House Buyer*, *Buying Your Home* and *Home Finder* which are useful if you are looking for a new house on an estate. So go down to your newsagent and buy all they have got – you probably will not need more than one copy of each of the monthly magazines as the advertisements tend to be from the same builders. If there does not seem much property available you might consider inserting a 'Property Wanted' advert in a local newspaper.

Never agree to pay an estate agent commission to find you a house – it is the seller who employs an estate agent and it is he who should pay him. If you write to an agent just ask for details of available property of the type you want – do not let him think you have commissioned him to find a house for you (for which he might insist on charging you).

Get yourself a map of the area before you start viewing – it will save you a lot of wasted time. Sometimes estate agents give them away free. Remember that it is an estate agent's job to make every house or flat seem as attractive as possible. The checklist below will help remind you of your needs – an estate agent will not tell you what the house lacks when you fall in love with the split level reception room and spiral staircase.

Checklist for house hunters

Number of bedrooms
Bathroom
Separate wc
Fitted kitchen, space for washing machine, drier, etc.
Size of sitting room
Separate dining room
Second bath and/or wc
Extra room, e.g. study, workroom, guest room
Garage, car port, parking space and parking for visitors
Garden, patio, terrace, balcony, space for greenhouse or garden shed, view from the kitchen window
Space for alterations or additions
Cupboards and storage space, warm linen cupboard
Central heating and hot water
Extras included, e.g. carpets, curtains, light fittings, fridge, cooker, TV aerial.
Convenience for public transport and shops

Before you step inside

Many is the time you will know that a house is not for you even before you have pressed the front door bell. Do not sneak away –

sellers get used to people who are not particularly interested and it is worth getting an idea of what is on offer and at what price.

You may even be able to save yourself a journey. First of all pinpoint the house on your map. Is it convenient for the bus route or close (but not too close) to the railway station? Is it too close to any likely sources of noise (e.g. school, pub, dance hall, sports club, main road, railway line, airport, police, fire or ambulance station, hospital with a casualty department, workshop or car repair yard) or to any unpleasant smell (e.g. farm, factory or stables). With both noise and smell the direction of the prevailing wind is important; if six out of seven days a week the smell or noise is blown in the opposite direction, it will not be such an inconvenience.

Does the house have a garage, car port, or space for off-street parking where you might build a garage later? Are the reception rooms of the house south facing? If they are north facing it will be a cold, dark place to live in. And is the garden likely to get much sun? Remember, the sun is much lower in winter than in summer, but if there are trees nearby they will look much smaller without leaves – and in summer, though decorative, will allow a lot less light through. Nearby buildings also cut off light – especially in the winter when the sun is low. They may also intrude on your privacy: can the garden or rooms in the house be seen into easily by passers-by or neighbours?

Once you are inside

Having pressed the door bell, you are then welcomed in. As you are shown round the house, look out for the points mentioned in the estate agent's blurb and do not be afraid to ask if something is not mentioned. You will soon learn to translate these blurbs: for 'compact' read 'very small'; for 'modern house' read 'built after World War I'; for 'period home' read 'a home which cannot be described in any other way'; and for 'defying any stream of superlatives', read 'nice, but costly'. It is not surprising that all estate agents' handouts contain a sentence disclaiming responsibility for the accuracy of the description or for any misrepresentation.

First impressions can often be good indications. Remember, the seller will have done his best to make the house as attractive as he can – you should be seeing it at its best. Is your immediate impression that it is poky, characterless or cold? If it is, the odds are you will not want to buy it. On the other hand property can look quite different at different times of day. If your first appointment is on a winter's afternoon or evening, make sure you go back and take a look when there is more natural light.

Even if your first impression is bad, it might not be anything a fresh coat of paint would not cure. As you look round, envisage where you would put your furniture. Will everything fit in? Where will the television set go? Is there a broom cupboard and enough kitchen cupboards and surfaces? Are the rooms an appropriate shape? Is it possible to get from the kitchen to the dustbin without walking through the main living room? Has the room you are likely to use most got a pleasant view? Does this room have direct access to the garden? If you have plans for children, would you be able to see them at play in the garden from the kitchen? Is there room for the kitchen appliances you have or might buy in the future? Would you have to keep the washing machine, dryer or freezer in the garage? If so, is there plumbing and electricity already laid on there? Is there central heating and does the boiler also heat the hot water? If applicable, where is the fuel stored? What type of fuel? What are the fuel bills? Is there mains gas, even if it is not currently used? What are the rates or community charge?

Are the carpets and curtains included? (Do not ask unless you want them.) Are light fittings, and for that matter anything screwed to the wall or ceiling, included? Ask specifically for any item you want and make a list of those that are included or agreed as extras. Also make a note whether the plumbing or electrical system is antiquated; if there are lead or iron pipes or round-pin sockets you are likely to be in for a pretty hefty plumbers' or electricians' bill in due course. If the house is in the country, check it is connected to the main sewer, and if not, check the costs, if any, of sewage disposal.

Always go into every room – even on to a balcony. It may seem much bigger than it really is. Is there room for a pram in the hall – if you need it? Is there anywhere to hang coats? Will your car fit into the garage with enough room to open the car door and get in and out? Has the house been well looked after? Has it been newly decorated – often a sign of cracked walls beneath? Are there signs of damp or bad condensation? (Look for stains above the skirting board or near the ceiling.) If enough things build up to put you off now, it is much better than getting cold feet about the deal after you have paid the cost of a surveyor and solicitor.

Ask why the sellers are moving. If they are similar to you in age and outlook and have been happy, but outgrown their home, then the odds are you will be happy too. If they appear to resent your reasonable questions, perhaps they have something to hide.

Ask about the neighbours: what do they do and how old are they? Young and old can mix very well, but this is not always the case. If possible, go and have a chat with them. They may tell you about any likely snags – for example, all the houses in the area are subsiding, or they have been campaigning to prevent a major road being built in the vicinity.

If you are buying a flat, listen for noise from the flats above, below and on either side. Ask the seller if this troubles him. Check the ceilings for stains or repairs, evidence of previous flooding. If it is a basement flat, check whether windows may be obscured by parked cars. Also ask about the cost of the service charge and if the landlord or his agent is efficient and pleasant.

Making an offer (except Scotland)[10]

When you find a house you like, do not be afraid to ask the people who are showing you round if you can talk privately for a minute or two with your partner to find out what you each think about it.

If you want to make an offer to buy, show both enthusiasm and reticence: enthusiasm to show that you are really serious and want to buy; reticence because you do not want the price to be raised – and perhaps you can even get it down a bit. A figure to aim for is 5% less. But play it by ear: do not hesitate to make an offer there and then if you really like the place. You cannot be held to anything you say verbally – a property contract must be in writing. If you prefer, you can make an offer through the seller's estate agent who will have experience in getting his clients to agree on a price.

If you do make an offer and it is accepted, make sure you give the seller your name, address and both daytime and evening telephone numbers. Give him the same details about your solicitor. Get the seller's full name, address and telephone number (day and evening) if you do not already have this information. And get details of his solicitor. In the case of solicitors, give and obtain the name of the person who will actually be dealing with the transaction.

Then write to the seller confirming your offer and his acceptance, but *make quite sure* that you include the words 'subject to contract' either immediately after your offer or at the top of the page. By doing this you can withdraw later without obligation. You can also add 'subject to survey' if you wish. You might also want to send a copy to the seller's estate agent to discourage him from sending more people to look round.

Specify everything which the seller has agreed to include in the sale – curtains, carpets, fitted cupboards, light fittings, television aerial. Some sellers have an unfortunate habit of asking for more money for such extras if it is not made clear from the start what is included. Ring up your solicitor and send him a similar letter telling him the name and address of the seller and his solicitor. This will start the legal process described in Chapter 7.

At this stage the estate agent may ask for a deposit. This is not necessary, and your best tactic is to refer him to your solicitor. If he insists on a deposit before the contract is signed, make sure he is reputable, i.e. he belongs to one of the recognised estate agents' organisations or tell him you will pay it to the seller's solicitor. In either case you should send a letter with the deposit stating that it has been paid to a 'Stakeholder subject to contract'. If either side withdraws later before contracts have been exchanged, you are entitled to a full refund.

At a sale by auction, a spoken offer is binding if accepted by the auctioneer. Once the auctioneer's hammer has fallen to the highest bid, he is authorised to make a binding contract on your behalf and you must pay him a 10% deposit there and then. So you need to find out all about the house, have it surveyed and so on, before the auction takes place. If you subsequently withdraw, you lose your deposit.

Gazumping

Having stressed the importance of making your initial offer 'subject to contract', so that you can withdraw later without obligation, it should not surprise you that the seller can do the same. At times when prices are rising and there is a lot of demand for property, a 'sellers' market' may develop, and the seller may receive other offers almost as soon as he has received yours. If you have offered him less than the asking price, it would seem reasonable that he accepts yours subject to someone else coming along and offering him his advertised price. Unless the seller instructs him not to do so, an agent is under a legal obligation to pass on all offers he receives until contracts have been exchanged.

Gazumping describes the situation where you have made an offer, usually at the full asking price, but later the seller decides that he wants more money from you. This may be because he has had another, higher offer from someone else or he may just think you are very keen and might be prepared to pay him more. The gazumper usually gives the impression that he is going to sell to you but then shortly before contracts are exchanged and after you have incurred legal, survey and other expenses, he insists you pay a few hundred or even a few thousand pounds more. If you do not agree, he says he will sell to someone else.

Gazumping became a common phrase in England in 1972 when the practice of raising the asking price after a 'subject to contract' offer had been accepted became epidemic in some parts of the country. (The expression gazumping is used in the United States to describe the sharp practices of second-hand car dealers.)

However, when demand for property declines and mortgages are in very short supply, gazumping quickly fades away. And then it may occasionally be replaced by the reverse practice of a buyer pushing the price down when a seller is desperate to be rid of a slowly moving property.

House chains

When homes are difficult to sell, sometimes your purchase may be held up because the person you are buying from can't move into his new home, because the person he is buying from can't move into his new one, and so on. It can happen that three, six or even more transactions, all depending on one another, can be held up by someone along the 'chain' either not being able to obtain a mortgage, or not being able to sell their home. Once the broken link in the chain finds a mortgage or buyer, then all the other transactions can get moving.

Surveyors and hazards

When you buy a home on a mortgage, the lender always instructs a surveyor to inspect the home and prepare a valuation. The lender gets a written report, and nowadays most building societies will let you see the report, which you have to pay for. The lender's valuation may show that a home is in bad condition, but it is mainly to indicate whether it provides sufficient security for the lender.

It is therefore important for you to get a surveyor to inspect your prospective home on your own account, in the hope of discovering any structural defects, like rising damp, rot, subsidence, or a worn out roof, before you buy. You should be able to get the same person to do your lender's valuation as well as your survey. This will cost you less than getting your own survey for the structural survey and paying separately for a lender's valuation. A survey and valuation from a building society naturally costs more than if you just have the valuation done. Societies vary in what they charge for these reports; some have three levels of thoroughness with prices to match.

If you decide to get an independent surveyor, choose a building surveyor who belongs to the Royal Institution of Chartered Surveyors (who will have FRICS or ARICS after his name), or the Incorporated Society of Valuers and Auctioneers. Your best bet is to get a personal recommendation from someone you know who has used a surveyor in the same area. Local knowledge can be important in surveying; for example, areas affected by mining subsidence will be well known locally but might be missed by an outsider. There are surveyors in independent practice and these might be worth trying in preference to those tied up with an estate agency.

It is best to get a list of three or four names and ring round and discuss your requirements. They will want to know the approximate size of the house, and where it is, and should be able to give you a quote there and then. Once you know their fees, choose the one you judge is likely to do the best job if there is not too much difference in what they charge. When you commission the surveyor, ask for a 'full structural survey'. There is no point in his supplying measurements of rooms – so it is worth telling him you do not want them.

If you are buying a flat or maisonette, instruct the surveyor to assess the state of the whole building as well as your flat. The flat may be fine – but if the roof or foundations are rotten there could be an extremely high maintenance charge on its way. You might be able to save money if the building society surveyor agrees to do a full structural survey at the same time as he does his inspection for the society. Surveyors who belong to the professional bodies mentioned above have errors and omissions insurance to cover them if they miss something and you have to sue them.

What surveyors look for

It is possible to save yourself the cost of a survey if you can spot a property in poor condition before you call in a surveyor. If the house has old round-pin sockets you can be sure that it needs to be rewired. Even if the plugs look new, if some of the wires seem old or are laid on the surface, you should add the cost of rewiring to your budget. The same applies if you see old lead or cast iron pipes; copper or plastic are likely to have been installed more recently.

With other faults it is more difficult to judge whether they should deter you from buying or not. Like many professional people, surveyors can disagree on the importance of defects. Evidence of rising damp is not necessarily a reason not to buy; the question to ask is whether it can be treated easily and without undue expense.

Damage or leaks in a roof may not be serious; but if a leak has been neglected there may be rot which, if extensive, can cost a lot of money to put right.

Condensation is often a problem which is not readily cured. If there are damp patches which are explained as 'only condensation', take care, as curing condensation can sometimes be more difficult than coping with rising damp.

If you are worried about subsidence, it is pointless to search for cracks; if there is serious subsidence the seller will almost certainly have filled them in. Instead, ask whether the house is built on old mine workings or clay, both likely causes of subsidence; and be wary if there are young trees growing close to the house, especially if they are on someone else's property.

Surveyors seem to have widely differing views on the quality of brickwork. So don't be put off if you get a report that says the house needs completely repointing – it may well last another five or even seven years without attention!

Do not be too easily put off by a pessimistic survey report. Provided the building society is still prepared to lend, a bad survey report is a means of knocking the price down – or getting the seller to do repairs before he leaves. Always remember, the seller is usually as anxious to sell as you are to buy.

If a surveyor does not follow your instructions, for example if you ask him specifically to inspect the foundations and he does not, do not pay him in full – or make him go back and finish the job.

The surveyor's report should advise you of any additional tests he considers necessary (e.g. rot, woodworm, wiring or drains). But there are a large number of reputable woodworm and rising damp and dry rot specialists who do inspections and provide written reports free of charge.[11] If the house is old it is worth having one of these as an added protection; again try and get someone to recommend a firm they have used and been pleased with. You have to pay extra for an electrician to test the wiring, or for a builder to test the drains.

If you need to have work done, make sure you get more than one quote; estimates can vary enormously, in one case from £135 to £674 for the same job.

Before you move in

Ask the person whom you are buying from to leave instruction booklets for any fixtures and gadgets they are leaving (e.g. central heating, built-in cooker, swimming pool). It could also be useful to know where the water stopcock is.

Notes

1 *Housing Research Unit*, University of Surrey, 1978.
2 For further information, contact the Society of Self Builders.
3 For further advice get *Condensation*, Advisory Leaflet No. 61, Department of Environment/PSA, HMSO.
4 Get the free booklets: *What Buildmark means to you*, National House-Building Council.
5 See free leaflet *Leasehold Reform*, Department of Environment, Welsh Office. Whilst you have no right to buy the freehold of a flat, you could negotiate with the landlords to buy the freehold of the whole block, either by yourself or by a company with shares owned by some or all of the residents. The Federation of Private Residents Association provides help in setting up such companies.
6 You can buy them out under the Rent Charges Act, 1977. See free

leaflets *Rent Charges*, *Apportionment of Rents*, Rent Charges Act, 1977; *Redemption Rent Charges*, Department of Environment.

7 *Feu duty* in Scotland is an annual payment similar to a ground rent. No new *feu duties* can be created, and existing *feu duties* must be redeemed by the vendor on a sale. See Tenure Reform (Scotland) Act, 1974.

8 *Mobile Homes: A guide for residents and site owners*, Department of Environment, Welsh Office.

9 For addresses see free leaflet *Buying or Selling a House?*, Law Society of Scotland.

10 This section on making an offer does not apply to Scotland – for what to do there see the appropriate part of Chapter 7.

11 For example, members of the British Wood Preserving Association, British Chemical Dampcourses Association. The Guarantee Protection Trust provides insurance if the company doing your treatment goes out of business before the guarantee expires.

3

Buying Your Council House or Flat

If you live in a council house or flat, is it worthwhile buying the home you live in? Under the provisions of the 1980 and 1983 Housing Acts,[1] most council tenants have the right to buy the house or flat they live in, and several hundred thousand have bought their homes. They also have the right to buy the home at a discount, ranging from 32% to 60%,[2] depending on the length of time they have spent as a council tenant. It is this discount which makes buying a council house or flat especially attractive. The 32% discount applies to tenants who have lived in a council house for two full years. The discount increases by 1% for each additional complete year, up to a maximum of 60% after thirty years as a tenant. For council flats the discounts are even higher – 44% after two years, increasing by 2% a year to 70% after fifteen years as a tenant.

People who have done it

Since 1970 some councils have been selling their property to tenants on a reasonably large scale and have given discounts ranging from 20 to 50%. A very common experience was that at the beginning the tenants who became homeowners had considerably higher accommodation costs than their neighbours. In one case the mortgage payments came to more than twice their weekly rent – and they had to pay rates on top, previously included in the rent. But five years later, their neighbour's rent had doubled – and their mortgage payments, allowing for tax relief plus rates, were about the same as their neighbour's rent.[3]

How long it takes for council rents to catch up with mortgage payments depends on the rate of increase of either: in recent years both have shown a tendency to rise and rise. But mortgage payments can go down – council rents never do.

If you are older – and therefore choose to repay your mortgage over a shorter period of time (say ten to fifteen years instead of twenty-five years) – this will make the mortgage payments higher, and therefore delay the time when you are better off than your neighbours. There is no reason, however, why an older tenant should not take an interest only, or standing mortgage, with the mortgage being repaid when the home is sold after the owner dies.

Reselling

Most council tenants who buy do so not because they want to be self-reliant in retirement, but because they want to own their own home and have the freedom which goes with it.[4] The snag about buying a council house or flat is that it may not be as readily resaleable if it is situated on an estate which has remained predominantly council. This may depend on the characteristics of the estate – and it might be argued that it is not the fact that the estate is a council one, but rather the design and scale which puts off would-be buyers who are not already living there. However, Government proposals for regenerating inner city housing estates may make council estates more attractive than they have been in the past. There is no doubt that if the estate where you buy is small or close to the countryside, you will have less trouble. Of course if you happen to live in an isolated council house, not on a council estate at all, then no one will even know it used to be a council house.

In some cases, even if there is prejudice against buying a house on a council estate, this may be remedied if a majority of tenants decide to buy. This is more likely to occur where the estate is a modern and pleasant one.

If you decide to sell the council house or flat you have bought at a discount within three years, you will have to refund part of the discount. If you sell after one year, you must refund 66⅔% of the discount; after two years 33⅓%. After three years as an owner you can sell without refunding any of the discount.

The right to buy

The right to buy applies to a 'secure' council tenant who has been one for a total of two years – not necessarily continuously – before an application to purchase.[5] The rules apply to local councils, new town development corporations and some housing associations. A local council can sell a home to anyone else – but only 'secure' tenants can compel the council to do so.

Most council tenancies are 'secure' tenancies. Exceptions include fixed term tenancies for more than twenty-one years (which is more like owning than renting anyway); tenancies where the home goes with a job (e.g. school caretakers); temporary accommodation for the homeless and private sector tenants whose homes are being repaired; tenancies on land which the council acquired for development; business and licensed tenancies; tenancies to students and tenancies of less than a year provided for people who move into an area to take up an employment offer; and licences held by people who originally were squatters.

When you have a joint tenancy, both partners have a joint right to buy. In addition, the tenant buying is allowed to buy jointly with up to three members of his family who have been living with him continuously for at least twelve months at the time he applies to buy the house or flat.

Almost all council and new town houses and flats are included in the scheme. Flats and maisonettes are sold on a 125 year lease, and service charges and the cost of repairs are passed on to residents in the same way as in private blocks of flats (see Chapter 9). A tenant who wants to buy his own flat may be offered another flat by the local council instead: this could be to his advantage if the council intends to put all its purchasers into one block – and to sell off complete blocks rather than leaving a mixture of council tenants and owner-occupiers which might otherwise be the case.

Tenants of certain accommodation for the elderly or disabled which has been purpose built or specially converted do not have the right to buy although councils can sell this sort of accommodation if they wish.

Special conditions may apply when a council sells a house in an area of Outstanding Natural Beauty or National Park, or certain other rural areas; any subsequent sale might be restricted to someone who has lived or worked there for, say, three years. Other conditions may also be applied. In such areas, if the purchaser wants to sell within ten years, he may have to offer it back to the council at the current market price, as judged by the District Valuer.

The market value of the house or flat is worked out by the local council – but the tenant has the right to appeal to the District Valuer if he thinks the value put on his home is too high. The valuation usually applies to the date of the tenant's application to buy.

Mortgages and options

There is no reason why you have to get your mortgage from the council just because you are a council tenant buying a council house or flat. In fact the Government wants to encourage building societies to lend on council homes. However, council tenants up to the age of 60, in England and Wales, have the right to a mortgage from the council of not less than two and a half times the tenant's income (plus one times the income of each other purchaser), or 100% of the purchase price if this is less. Tenants over the age of 60 have lower multiples of income, reducing as they get older. Joint mortgages are available with up to three other members of the household. All these mortgages can be for twenty-five years. In Scotland the right to a council mortgage is available following a refusal by a building society.

If a tenant cannot get a large enough mortgage, he or she can take an option to purchase the home at any time from two years following the date of the initial application at the same price. The option requires a £100 returnable deposit.

Shared ownership

Suppose you cannot afford the deposit or payments on your home. Why not buy half or a third instead? This seemingly 'pie in the sky' solution has been used since 1975 by Birmingham City Council which sold new houses not only to tenants but also to would-be owner-occupiers who are not. Shared ownership schemes may become more common in the future as some of the obstacles to them have been removed. Since 1983, council tenants who cannot afford to buy outright have the right to buy on a shared ownership basis.

The most important feature of shared ownership is that the purchaser has the option to buy the remainder once he can afford to do so. The value at which this is done will be the market value at the time the option is exercised. Whatever proportion is bought, the purchaser will be regarded as an owner rather than a tenant and thus has the rights and obligations of an owner even though his share may be less than 50%. Shared ownership purchases are made on a 99 or 125 year lease – though once the option to buy the remaining half has been taken up, the purchaser of a house will be able to obtain the freehold.[6]

Notes

1 This applies to England and Wales. Similar provisions apply to Scotland and are contained in Tenants' Rights, Etc. (Scotland) Act 1980.

2 There is a maximum value of discount of £25,000. Also the discounted sale price of a house must not be less than the costs incurred after 31 March 1974 of providing, improving or repairing the house.

3 *Daily Mail*, 28 March 1979.

4 For how tenants can swap accommodation see Appendix 1.

5 For how to set about buying the home, see the free leaflet *Your Right to Buy Your Home*, Department of Environment, Welsh Office, Scottish Information Office. You also need a 'Right to Buy' Claim Form.

6 There is a free leaflet *Local Authority Shared Ownership*, Department of Environment, Welsh Office.

4

Initial Costs

In addition to finding a mortgage there are a number of other costs you will incur when buying a property. Many of these are related to the purchase price and in this chapter I have illustrated these with the example of a couple buying their first home for £40,000.

Deposit

It is uncommon to obtain a mortgage for 100% of the purchase price. Around 90% to 95% is a typical upper limit. So with a £40,000 house you might have to find a £2,000 to £5,000 deposit.

Solicitors' charges

There are no fixed scales of solicitors' fees. Although the Royal Commission on Legal Services reporting in October 1979 recommended that a maximum scale be introduced, this was not implemented. According to a report in *Which?* magazine in February 1986, legal charges have been falling. The magazine found a range from £100 to £450 plus VAT for buying a £45,000 house and selling a £35,000 house. In our example of a £40,000 house, the solicitor's fee comes to £200 plus VAT; £100 would be cheap, £400 expensive.

There may also be the lender's solicitor's fee for preparing the mortgage. Usually your own solicitor can act for both the lender and you, and quotes an inclusive fee as above. Some small building societies and foreign banks insist they are represented by a separate solicitor. If the same solicitor does not act for you, it will be more expensive. The lender's solicitor's charge could be half as much again as it would have been had he also been acting for you,[1] and your own solicitor may also charge a fee for dealing with the mortgage on your behalf. It will also slow things down.

The most effective way to keep a solicitor's charges down is to ask for a quote at the outset. The Law Society and the Law Society of Scotland supply solicitors with forms for giving estimates for conveyancing, which should set out all the costs the solicitor pays on your behalf as well as his own charges. Few solicitors will not be prepared to work on that basis, but they should at least give you an estimate, and only if your transaction turns out to be more time consuming are they entitled to charge more.

Ask more than one firm of solicitors what they would charge and make sure that they include the cost of dealing with the mortgage for both you and the lender. Ask what the stamp duty and land registry fees would be (see below). Also ask whether the estimate includes VAT. You should then have a comprehensive and accurate guide to the expense involved. Unless the differences are small, go to the cheapest.

If a solicitor refuses to give you any idea of the cost, go elsewhere. There is most scope for shopping around if you are buying or selling an expensive house – there is no more work, but many solicitors tend to relate the fee to the value of the house. Some solicitors advertise how much they charge in the 'For Sale' columns of local or national newspapers. Make sure there are no hidden snags like having to take an expensive mortgage through them.

Once you have agreed terms with a solicitor, it is best to confirm them in writing so there can be no misunderstanding. Other ways of saving on legal costs are to go to cut-price conveyancing firms or to do the conveyancing yourself. These are discussed in Chapter 7.

When the transaction is completed, sometimes a solicitor charges more than his estimate. If this account exceeds the estimate by a significant amount, say £50 or more, ring him up and ask him why – if he has not already explained. In England and Wales[2] if you are not satisfied with his answer, do not pay the bill, but instead write to your solicitor requesting that he obtain a Remuneration Certificate from the Law Society. If you do this, the solicitor sends the papers to the Law Society which certifies either that the bill is reasonable or else fixes a *lower* sum. If you pay the bill you lose your rights to have the Law Society check the bill unless the solicitor deducts his charges from any money he owes you. You can ask for a Remuneration Certificate even if the solicitor does not exceed his estimate if you think you have been overcharged. In 1976 the Law Society said they reduced about a quarter of the bills sent to them, but most people did not query their bills. If the solicitor's bill is not reduced, you have to pay interest on the unpaid bill from the time it was due until the time you pay it.

Land registry fees

In England and Wales most houses are now registered at one of the regional land registries or will have to be registered when you buy. When a registered house or flat is transferred (or first registered), fees have to be paid by the purchaser, and the solicitor pays them on your behalf. This adds another £100 to our specimen bill; the more expensive the property, the larger the fee. At the time of writing, land registry fees amounted to roughly ¼% of the purchase price on a transfer.

The fees for a first registration are lower in England and Wales (higher in Scotland) – but your solicitor will have more work so he

Table 5 Check list of costs for £40,000 purchase with £35,000 mortgage

		Your cost £	*Example* £
1	Your deposit	.....	5,000
2	Solicitor's charge[1]	.....	230
3	Land registry fees	.....	100
4	Stamp duty	.....	400
5	Valuation and survey cost[1]	.....	172
6	Removal expenses[1]	.....	200
7	Decorating, repairs etc.[2]	.....	400
8	Furniture, carpets etc.[1]	.....	2,000
9	Anything else[3]	.....	
	Total funds you need in addition to mortgage	.....	8,502

[1]Including VAT at 15%.
[2]Assuming you do a lot yourself.
[3]For example: estate agent's charges if you are selling as well as buying.

may charge more than he otherwise would. No land registry fee is payable to register a mortgage taken out at the same time as a purchase. A solicitor should be able to tell you how much the land registry fees will be. There is no VAT on land registry fees.

Stamp duty

Stamp duty is payable to the Inland Revenue by purchasers on the whole value of the property where the purchase is above certain limits. These limits are changed from time to time; and the announcement is usually made in the budget. From 14 March 1984 no stamp duty is payable on properties bought for £30,000 or less; from £30,001 upwards the rate is 1%

If the asking price is near this limit, try and bargain the price down. For instance if the price is £30,950 and you get it down to £30,000, you need pay nothing instead of £309. Check with your solicitor what the correct rates are at the time you are buying.

There is no stamp duty payable on moveable things you buy with the house – fittings, carpets, etc. – if you agree a separate price for them. In such a situation you should ask your solicitor to suggest the seller agrees to 'apportion' the price; so you might pay £30,000 for the house – and £950 for fixtures, carpets, etc. Stamp duty would then amount to nothing, i.e. the same as on a £30,000 purchase.

There is no stamp duty if you exchange your home with a builder or another person. If there is a cash payment to make up for the difference in value, there is only stamp duty on this cash amount – and none if it is £30,000 or less.

If you buy a plot of land for £30,000 or less and then get a builder to build a home costing £60,000 on the site, there is no stamp duty either. Alternatively, buy a half-built house for £30,000 or less and pay the builder to finish it and you avoid stamp duty.

Inspection, valuation and survey fees

Before the building society even offers you a loan, it will want a cheque for its inspection or valuation fee. This is on a scale based on the price of the house – not the amount of the loan. The only scope to haggle with the building society over this is if the mortgage is a very low proportion of the price – say less than a third.

Banks may let you get your own valuation and survey, in which case you pay the surveyor direct.

I recommend you combine the valuation and survey (see p. 26 for advice on choosing a surveyor). This might cost you £172 including VAT on a £40,000 house.

Removal, decorations, furniture

Allow another £100 to £300 for removal expenses. Even if you do it yourself you will probably have to hire a van and throw a house warming party for the friends who helped you; also make sure you are insured for breakages in transit, although they may be less likely to occur if you are doing it yourself. If you employ a professional firm you will pay less if you do your own packing. Get quotes from two or three firms and compare them with the cost (and trouble) of doing it yourself.

You will probably want to redecorate inside and perhaps outside. Even a place which looks quite clean with its old furniture in place tends to look rather shabby after the pictures have been taken off the walls. And unless it is a new house the surveyor may find repairs which need to be seen to. Indeed, the building society may insist on these being done as a condition of the loan. £400 is allowed for this in our example, which must assume you will be doing most of it yourself.

You may also find that once you get your own home you want to buy a lot of 'once and for all' items which now seem essential but which you never thought you would need when you rented or lived with your parents. A home has to be furnished. If you are lucky you will buy one with fitted carpets and curtains which you like; these can be very valuable, as it costs at least £1,000 to carpet the average home. Sometimes even the cooker and fridge are left. You may get presents of course; and it is amazing what good value second-hand furniture can be if you just cannot afford new. Make sure you have at least £1,800 to spare (or a good credit limit on your credit card) to cope with this extra expenditure.

Add another £200 for the 'light fittings' which the seller in our example now says were not included originally – and our purchaser has to find a deposit for £8,502 – a lot more than the £5,000 first thought of. My figures are just an example, of course – so you should carefully work out for yourself what your initial costs will be.

Notes

1 The building society solicitor's fee is a scale between the Law Society and the Building Societies' Association. The scale and other costs are published by the latter in a free booklet *Starting Point*.

2 If you are dissatisfied with a Scottish solicitor's charges you are entitled to have his bill submitted to 'taxation' by the Auditor of the Court of Session (even after you have paid it) but you will have to pay the cost of the taxation and the Auditor can raise the bill as well as lower it.

5

Finding a Mortgage

A mortgage is a loan secured on your home. If you do not repay the loan in the way you have agreed, the lender can apply to a Court to sell your property to get his money back.

Building societies provide around three-quarters of mortgages for owner-occupation, in some years as many as nine out of ten, but since 1981 banks have also offered mortgages to their customers. Other lenders are local councils and insurance companies. Some first time buyers buy their home without a mortgage.

Choosing a building society

Many building societies will only lend to people who have invested their savings with them, especially when funds are in short supply, as they often are. So if you think you might want a mortgage, you would be wise to plan in advance and keep as much money as you can in one or more building societies. Preferably more than one, because some societies are fussier than others about the type of property on which they lend. Also, when funds are in short supply they ration them in different ways. There is no point, however, in spreading your money too thinly or at the last minute – if your account has only £50 in it, or you have only had it a few months, no society will be impressed. What they like to see is regular saving or large balances. So you could save regularly with one society – subscription accounts pay high interest rates – and keep any lump sum you have in an instant access account with another.

Nowadays most building societies have leaflets which summarise their mortgage terms – it is well worth while getting hold of a copy before you start saving. These rules do change from time to time however. One couple I heard of moved all but £20 of their savings from one building society to another because they discovered they could get a larger loan provided they saved for six months. At the end of six months they were aghast to discover that the new society had changed its rules – and would now only lend to investors who had been with them for eighteen months. They went back to the first society, which fortunately offered them the mortgage they needed. Their attempt to beat the system had done them no good at all.

The twenty largest building societies at the time of writing are: Halifax, Abbey National, Nationwide Anglia, Alliance & Leicester, Woolwich, Leeds Permanent, National & Provincial, Bradford & Bingley, Britannia, Cheltenham & Gloucester, Bristol & West, Yorkshire, Birmingham-Midshires, Northern Rock, Town & Country, Coventry, Chelsea, Skipton, Leeds & Holbeck, Guardian.

Choosing a bank

When the banks began to lend money for mortgages they were prepared to lend to anyone. When they cut back a bit, they restricted their lending to existing bank customers (e.g. people with current, cheque-book accounts) of at least six months' standing. If you are contemplating getting a mortgage in the future, you should open a current account with one of the banks which grants mortgages. Banks which have granted mortgages are: Barclays, Clydesdale, Co-operative, Girobank, Lloyds, Midland, National Westminster, Royal Bank of Scotland, Trustee Savings Banks (TSB), and Yorkshire Bank. If you get a mortgage from a bank you will normally be expected to move your current account to it if you are not already a customer.

Homeloan scheme

This scheme was introduced by the Government in 1978 and anyone who has never owned a home before (i.e. any prospective first time buyer) should pick up the appropriate notification form and join. Savings under the scheme need not be newly commenced nor be with a building society – National Savings Bank, bank deposit accounts and National Savings Index-Linked SAYE also qualify. After two years in the scheme, when you apply for a mortgage (which does not have to be from the institution with which you have registered), you should be able to benefit from an extra tax free grant of between £40 and £110, and an extra loan of up to £600 on which you will not have to pay interest or repay any capital for the first five years. The main snag is that your home must cost less than a figure from a regional list, which is updated from time to time. The limits are given in Table 6. If your home costs more than the figure for your region, you will not qualify.

Table 6 Homeloan scheme (limits from 18 March 1988)

England		
Greater London		£63,000
South East	*Bedfordshire, Berkshire, Buckinghamshire, Essex, Hampshire, Hertfordshire, Isle of Wight, Kent, Oxfordshire, Surrey, Sussex*	£51,800
South West	*Avon, Cornwall, Devon, Dorset, Gloucestershire, Somerset and Wiltshire; and the Isles of Scilly*	£38,300
East Anglia	*Cambridgeshire, Norfolk, Suffolk*	£38,400
East Midlands	*Derbyshire, Leicestershire, Lincolnshire, Northants, Nottinghamshire*	£30,300
West Midlands	*Hereford and Worcester, Shropshire, Staffordshire, Warwickshire, West Midlands*	£28,300
Yorkshire & Humberside	*Humberside, Yorkshire*	£25,800
North West	*Cheshire, Greater Manchester, Lancashire, Merseyside*	£26,800
Northern	*Cleveland, Cumbria, Durham, Northumberland, Tyne and Wear*	£26,600
Scotland		£30,400
Wales		£27,200
Northern Ireland		£26,300

Also you need to have £600 in the account when you ask for the mortgage, and an average of £300 over the previous twelve months to get the £40 grant, rising to £1,000 for the maximum grant. But it costs nothing to join – and the conditions may have varied by the time you come to buy your home. It is therefore well worth joining, you can lose nothing even if you do not eventually qualify. There is a free explanatory leaflet.

If you qualify by having had a savings account with enough money in it but have omitted to register under the Homeloan Scheme, you can backdate the registration. Building societies usually ask on their application form whether you have registered under the scheme. If you say you have not, they are unlikely to allow that you thought you were registered. To apply for the late entry application, ask the lender for Form HPA5 Failure to Notify. You have to declare that you have been saving with the intention of qualifying under the House Purchase Assistance Scheme and that you were not aware of the requirement to notify at the time you started saving. Form HPA3 is used to apply for the grant and extra loan.

If you qualify under this scheme, make sure your payments do not include interest or repayment on the extra £600 loan. Some building societies have been unable to teach their computers to cope with this, and borrowers have sometimes been asked to make payments which are not due.

How much they will lend you

You will usually be lent a multiple of your earnings before tax. If you receive regular spare-time earnings or overtime, the lender may also be prepared to take these into account – but will want proof. If you or your spouse have investment income – and are not going to put all the capital into the house purchase – this may also be taken into account. The multiple is often two and a half times your income; it could be as low as two or as high as three times your income. So if your income is £8,000 a year, you should be able to borrow between £16,000 and £24,000. When interest rates are high, the multiple tends to be lower.

Two incomes

Many young couples buy their first home when they are both earning. While two lenders may give the same amount to a sole earner, there is less uniformity when there are two. The Sex Discrimination Act 1975 makes it unlawful for mortgage lenders to discriminate against women. And nowadays it should be no more difficult for a single woman to get the mortgage she wants than a single man. Where the wife has higher earnings than the husband, couples should be offered as much as they would be if their earning capacities were reversed.

With two earners, lenders do not usually just add the incomes together. They may offer two and a half times the higher income, plus one times the lower. Or they may have another formula, say three times the higher plus half the lower. Sometimes they may add them together, but then just multiply them by one and a half or two. These different rules mean that, depending on the actual earnings of each partner, one lender may be prepared to give a higher mortgage than another.

Whether or not there are two earners, should you have large hire purchase or credit card commitments, other existing debts, pay maintenance to a separated or former wife, or have to support children who are not living with you, you might be offered less. So do not necessarily volunteer this information; if you are asked, as you often will be, you must of course tell the truth. Regular spare-time earnings or overtime ought to be taken into account but sometimes will not be – it rather depends on what the lender knows about the type of job you are in.

Most lenders will accept two single people as joint owners. Two couples who want to share a house in joint ownership should also be able to get a mortgage, but lenders may be wary of groups of more than two single people sharing.

Self-employed

The self-employed may find greater difficulty in getting a large enough mortgage in inflationary times. This is because most societies require to see the last three years' audited accounts – and some may take an average of them – a much more conservative basis than for an employed person. Someone who has recently set up in business on his own will find it difficult – even impossible – to get a building society mortgage unless a relative can offer a guarantee. People who run family businesses through a company may find societies less willing to accept their salary in full.

Do not overstretch yourself

Having given advice on how to set about getting the highest possible mortgage, it is appropriate here to warn about the dangers of overstretching yourself. Any house purchaser should always keep some cash in reserve for unforeseen eventualities.

You should also be careful not to offer evidence of overtime earnings if there is a chance your overtime might dry up – or worse, if you are in line to lose your job. Lenders make the loans based on a maximum multiple of your income for the very good reason that they have found from experience that on a lower income people often cannot afford the mortgage payments.

Remember also, if your wife is earning but is likely to stop work to have a baby before long, that is going to reduce your income sharply. There can also be a danger in taking on too large a loan when the mortgage interest rate is low. If it subsequently rises sharply you may not be able to afford the payments.

Building society and bank managers have discretion to vary the rules a bit – but for first time buyers it is often not their income which determines how much they can borrow, but the property they have chosen.

How much they will lend on the property

You may have worked out that your income is ample to support a mortgage of the amount you need. But if the loan you seek is over 80% of the price you are paying, you may hit another snag.

Lenders always make an inspection and valuation; sometimes this valuation is less than the price you have agreed to pay. For instance, although you might think you have a bargain at £40,000, the building society valuer may well reckon the value is £38,000. Most societies have a lending limit in terms of the percentage of valuation above which they will not lend. The £35,000 our example couple needs is 92% of the £38,000 at which the Heartless Society's surveyor valued their intended home. But Heartless applies its 90% lending limit and offers £34,200 – that is, 90% of the valuation.

The lending limit tends to vary according to the age, state of repair and type of house. Some societies lend lower proportions on more expensive houses. For houses built before 1920 this limit can be as low as 70% of valuation; for modern houses it can range from 85–100%. Mortgages of 100% of the purchase price are most likely when the purchaser is buying for less than the valuation: a sitting tenant could be in such a position (see Appendix 1).

Disliked property

Building societies used to seem to be against certain types of property, although the societies do vary in outlook. Banks seem less fussy. Converted flats used to be almost impossible to get building society mortgages on; now there are few societies which actually refuse point blank.

Some (but by no means all) building societies do not like houses without gardens, especially front gardens, though a small patio may be acceptable and flats without gardens are fine. Others will not lend on homes partially occupied by sitting tenants, or on homes without bathrooms (some will not lend even if you agree to put one in) or on homes with outside toilets only. 'Back-to-back' houses are frowned upon, and flats with only one bedroom, or even only one room, may not appeal to some lenders, although some firms of builders are now building these as new 'starter' homes for single people.

Leasehold property is expected to have a lease with from twenty to thirty years still to run *after* you have paid off the mortgage, i.e. a minimum forty-five to fifty-five years in total, in the case of a standard twenty-five year mortgage. It is difficult to get mortgages for freehold flats in England and Wales, because there cannot be enforceable agreements between the residents on how repairs, maintenance, etc., are carried out, and who pays for them.

Where a property is in need of fairly substantial repairs, a lender may withhold some of the loan. This is called a 'retention' and will generally amount to the estimated cost of the repairs which you need to carry out. Should the repairs be very extensive – a new roof, say – then the society withholds the whole loan until the repairs are completed. In either case a bank would normally be prepared to provide a bridging loan once you are able to show them a formal written offer from the building society.

If you are building your own home, make sure you arrange your eventual mortgage before you start building. You may have to do the initial construction with a bank bridging loan.

Additional security

As well as lending only to a maximum percentage of the valuation, banks and building societies also have a limit above which they require extra security. Usually this applies to any loan in excess of 80% of their valuation. In the case of a building society, this security can be one of the following:

1 A special insurance policy called a mortgage indemnity or guarantee policy which costs you 2% to 4½% of the amount in excess of 80%. The cost of the mortgage indemnity policy can usually be added to your loan – it is a single non-recurring premium. For example, you need a mortgage indemnity policy to cover the difference between £40,000 (80% of the society's £50,000 valuation) and £44,000 which you are borrowing. The cost is, say, 3% of £4,000 – that is, £120 – which the lender adds to their loan. This policy is completely different from a mortgage protection policy – see Chapter 6.
2 You could instead use a life insurance policy which has been going long enough to have a surrender value to cover the £4,000 above 80% which needs extra security. Young people often have such policies but they frequently do not have a large enough combined surrender value.
3 A mortgage on another property. This might cost as much in extra legal and land registry fees as the mortgage indemnity policy – so check whether it is worthwhile. It also has the disadvantage of tying up the other property.
4 A guarantee from a local Council under the Housing Act 1980, intended for houses in need of improvement bought under the Right to Buy Scheme, specially built for first time buyers, and under shared ownership schemes.

Mortgage not big enough

Having got to the stage of being offered a building society mortgage, you may find you have still not got enough money. In Chapter 4, I set out a sample checklist of initial costs. You may have estimated you needed £8,502 in addition to the mortgage. But because of the lower valuation put on your house by the lender's valuer, you may need to find more money, maybe £2,000.

You try to get the price down but the sellers are not prepared to budge, having already come down £2,000. You do not like the idea of using up your entire credit card limit on furniture; you would like to go on holiday the year after you move – and without saving the credit card for that it would be impossible.

This is where endowment policies may prove useful. If you have been paying premiums for a few years, the insurance companies may well lend on the security of their policies. Alternatively, you could see your bank manager, offer the security of the policies and show him the letters from the insurance companies. The bank manager might lend more, and will take the insurance policies as security. A bank loan would normally have to be paid off within five years – whereas the insurance companies would have waited until the maturity of the policies. The alternative – of credit card or hire purchase for the furniture – would be much more expensive. A bank loan or insurance policy loan costs less interest and qualifies for tax relief (see Chapter 12).

For people who cannot offer security such as life insurance policies, shares or unit trusts, banks will often take a second mortgage as security for a 'top-up' loan. Some building societies and local councils may not allow you to do this.

A second mortgage is given where a lender is prepared to take your property as security, but agrees that the first mortgage should have priority if you do not keep up the payments. It is not as good security as a first mortgage, which is why a second mortgage will be at a higher rate of interest.

Insurance companies also provide quite a lot of top-up loans. The snag often is that they require you to take out and keep up an expensive insurance policy to cover not just the top-up portion which they are lending you, but also the amount lent by your building society. Such arrangements, particularly where the amount to be topped up is small in relation to the total loan, should be avoided if at all possible – they turn out very expensive. If you do resort to a top-up loan from an insurance company, ask whether the building society loan can be linked to a lower cost endowment policy. Not all companies give this choice, insisting you take a full with-profits or non-profit policy for the amount of the combined value of your building society and top-up loan. For an explanation of why a lower cost policy is preferable, see p. 61. Insurance companies require a second mortgage as well as these insurance policies.

A top-up loan as well as your mortgage will therefore be more costly than a single mortgage for the full amount and should be avoided if possible.

Other lenders

Local authorities

Local authority mortgages are often in short supply because the local authorities are restricted by the government as to how much they are allowed to lend.

Local authorities differ in their rules about where and to whom they will lend. The authority to enquire at is the one in which you currently live – and the one into which you are moving. In Northern Ireland, instead of local authorities, you apply to the Northern Ireland Housing Executive.

Local authorities tend to work out how much they will lend to you in a different way from most building societies – although the actual loan may be about the same. They reckon that your before-tax weekly income should be enough to cover your monthly outgoings i.e. your mortgage payments. Some other lenders may include ground rent, rates or even heavy hire purchase commitments in your monthly outgoings. If there are two incomes, the higher, and say half the lower, may be taken into account.

Local authority mortgages are intended for cheaper housing so there is usually a maximum price of home they will contemplate lending on. These limits are raised from time to time. They also tend to restrict loans to older (pre-1939) houses.

In fact the council tries to step in when building societies are not interested. Often a building society refusal to lend on a certain property is required before a council will consider lending. Interest rates are similar to those of building societies.

In times when councils are very short of mortgage funds, building societies have agreed to consider council nominations. However, this will not help with a property or a borrower unacceptable to a society as the building societies have not agreed to lower their standards for council nominations, although it could get you a loan from a building society which otherwise lends only to people who have savings with it (when you have not).

Insurance companies
You are more likely to get a top-up mortgage than a full loan from an insurance company. Either way it will turn out rather expensive for the reasons already given (explained further in Chapter 6). A mortgage or insurance broker is the best person to fix you up with an insurance company loan if you can find no cheaper means of financing your purchase. Mortgage brokers advertise in the For Sale columns of local and national newspapers. Several magazines (e.g. *Money Management*) carry out surveys of insurance company mortgages and top-up facilities.

Employers
Some employers offer their staff low-interest loans. This is most common in banks, insurance companies and building societies, for obvious reasons.

Many large companies also have arrangements for introductions to building societies and insurance companies which can help you jump a queue. Employees of people in the trade, such as solicitors, accountants and estate agents, will also find doors open more easily.

Builders
With new property, particularly estates of new houses, the builder or property developer may have a financial arrangement with a building society. This saves you the trouble of asking around, provided the building society will lend enough.

Guaranteed mortgages

Although saving or having an account at a bank or building society may raise your chances of getting a mortgage when they are in short supply, it does not guarantee you one. Several banks and the Bradford & Bingley Building Society operate a 'guaranteed' mortgage scheme where you save for a certain minimum period of time – usually one or two years – after which you are 'guaranteed' some multiple of your savings, provided that your income is high enough, and the home you want to buy is valuable enough, to sustain the loan.

Many banks and building societies now offer a 'mortgage certificate' saying how much they will lend you, which you can get when you start house hunting. This may make it easier to clinch a deal if you are competing with other purchasers for your dream home.

Speeding things up

The only way to ensure you get a mortgage for more or less the amount you want is never to give up. Even if you have made advance plans by spreading your savings between two building societies, do not hesitate to move the money away to a third if their response to your enquiry is more encouraging. But make sure you speak to the right person – if you do not think what you have been told sounds right, write and ask for a written explanation of why they cannot lend.

Using contacts

Apart from doing your own footwork from branch to branch, always take advantage of your contacts. Bank managers, estate agents, solicitors, accountants, insurance brokers and insurance company agents all have influence with building societies. They recommend people to deposit money and in return are given a quota to be lent to their clients. Often the client need not even have an account with the society. Try to make sure any promises made to you are of substance, and check whether they charge an arrangement fee.

Insurance brokers and agents will want you to take out an endowment policy, but solicitors will not necessarily. If you do take one, the solicitor may be prepared to cut his conveyancing fees to take into account the commission he received on the insurance policy. If you do not have your own solicitor, as well as considering his fees and whether you like him, it may be as important to choose one who can get you a mortgage.

Mortgage brokers

As their name implies, mortgage brokers are in business to get people mortgages. They are licensed by the Office of Fair Trading.

Especially when mortgages are in short supply, they undoubtedly perform a very useful task for those who otherwise could not find one. They will generally find you a mortgage and you will normally be expected to take an endowment mortgage. The commission on the endowment policy serves to pay the broker for his work.

Whether or not you should have an endowment mortgage is discussed in the next chapter. You should consider paying the broker a fee instead of taking an endowment mortgage, if you don't want an endowment mortgage. You should make sure you know what the fee is beforehand. A typical mortgage broker's fee will be around 2% to 4% of the mortgage plus VAT – so a £30,000 mortgage could cost you £690 upwards. But remember, if the broker found you a loan for £4,000 more than you could have got yourself, you will have to put down £4,000 less towards the deposit – and should not therefore begrudge him the money.

The broker may ask for a fee in advance. You should *not* agree to this – if pressed, offer a part payment. Remember, if you meanwhile find a loan elsewhere, and do not want the one he finds, the maximum he can charge by law is £3 if you do not take up his introduction within six months. Where the loan is over £15,000, the broker is entitled to charge you for any surveys, etc., which he has had done on your behalf.

Preferably deal with a mortgage broker who is also an Insurance Broker, whose firm is listed by the Insurance Brokers' Registration Council, or one which is a member of FIMBRA.

Bridging

Loans

Generally speaking, you are advised not to sign a contract to buy a new home before you have also signed to sell your old one.

If for some reason you do, and have to finalise the purchase of the new one before you have the proceeds from the old one, you will need a bridging loan. You may also need a bridging loan if there is some delay in getting your mortgage, or if the lender 'retains' some of the loan until you have done repairs.

There are also two situations where you may need a bridging loan to cover part or all of the deposit.

The first applies to first time buyers who are offered a mortgage of over 90% of the purchase price. They will need to pay a 10% deposit when the contract is signed, whilst their contribution to the purchase price of the home may only be, say, 5%. The lender will not part with any money until the deal is completed, usually a month later. In this case it is worth asking the vendor's solicitor to accept a smaller deposit.

The second occurs when you are selling as well as buying, but do not intend to put any capital into the new house other than what you are realising from the old one. Say you are selling for £30,000 and buying a new house for £40,000. You have to put up a £4,000 deposit – but that £4,000 is tied up in your old house. You will not normally be able to use the £3,000 deposit paid to your solicitor by the purchaser of your old house because he holds it as 'stakeholder' which means he cannot pass it on to you without permission from your purchaser – which is unlikely to be forthcoming.

In either of these cases you should go and see your bank manager. Be quite definite about how long you will require the loan – usually the shorter the period the easier it is. You may be surprised how accommodating bank managers can be.

Provided you have a solicitor acting for you, he can hold the deeds of one of your two houses 'to the order of the bank' and so give them security for your bridging loan. If you use a conveyancing company or are doing-it-yourself, a bridging loan will be more difficult to get.

Ask the bank manager what rate of interest he charges, and whether there is a fee as well. If there is, and the loan is for a short period, try bargaining with him on this. Should your bank manager not be amenable to a bridging loan, this could be the moment to change banks. The same applies if his fee is high; some banks do not charge fees for bridging loans – just interest. You do not get tax relief on a fee for a bridging loan – only on the interest. And remember, the fee will often be payable even if you do not take up the loan.

Deposit guarantee

An alternative to a bridging loan could be a deposit guarantee. Instead of paying the deposit, your solicitor guarantees the deposit to the solicitors of the people you are buying from. Your solicitor takes out an insurance policy which provides the money if for some reason the money is not forthcoming. Ask your solicitor for details. The scheme is run by Legal & Professional Indemnity Ltd.[1]

Note

1 Legal & Professional Indemnity Ltd, 3 Clanricarde Gardens, Tunbridge Wells, Kent TN1 1PE. Tel: 0892-862345.

6

Repaying a Mortgage

Why is it that some people seem to find repaying their mortgage such a financial burden whilst others seem to take it in their stride? The reason lies not in the size of the loan you get; you will not get much more than three times your income, however confident you are that you can afford the repayments. It lies in the type of mortgage you choose. For the same size of loan, you can find yourself paying widely different amounts each month. It is therefore crucial not to be persuaded into getting a more expensive mortgage than you need.

Interest rates

Hardly any lenders charge a fixed rate of interest for a mortgage – they can raise or lower it at a month's notice or without notice – although you do not necessarily need to alter your monthly payments at once. Local authorities often used to charge fixed rates of interest – this is no longer the case for new mortgages. Some insurance companies still offer fixed rates of interest; with others the rate is reviewed after five years. Sometimes builders offer a fixed or reduced interest rate for the first year (or two) of the mortgage.

Building societies now compete with each other and with the banks. The result is that mortgage rates vary, and the greatest competition is for larger loans, i.e. over £60,000. You should aim to get your mortgage from the bank or building society which offers the cheapest interest rate for your size of loan. Regular surveys are carried out in Blays Residential Mortgage Tables, available from many public libraries. There can be large differences in rates between the best and the worst: up to 1% or 2% a year.

Whilst you should certainly try and avoid paying a higher interest rate than you need, it is likely to be true that building societies charging higher rates will be less popular with borrowers; they will also be more popular with investors, because they pass on the higher rates of interest charged on loans to investors. As a result, societies charging higher interest may well not make you wait so long for your loan, or may be able to offer you a larger loan. A larger loan at a slightly higher rate of interest may well be cheaper overall than one at the normal rate plus a very expensive top-up loan.

True interest rate

Banks and building societies have different ways of working out their mortgage payments, but both are obliged by law to state a true interest rate, called the annual percentage rate of charge, or APR; building societies may also quote the APR. The APR takes into account the different methods of calculating payments. The quoted interest rate for most banks will seem higher than the quoted rate from building societies, the Trustee Savings Banks, the National Westminster Bank and the Co-operative Bank. The payments, and the true rate (APR), will probably be the same. As well as asking about the interest rate, it is well worth asking for a quotation of the actual monthly payment for your level of mortgage, and compare the figures you are given.

Endowment mortgages (explained later in this chapter) used to be more expensive, ¼%, ½%, or 1% more. For new mortgages there is rarely an extra charge, and a few lenders charge less, say ½% less, for an endowment. There are often special offers where a low interest rate – say ¼% or ½% less than normal – is offered to first time buyers or people who want large mortgages for the first three years of the mortgage.

Interest rate changes

As the interest on a new mortgage is generally not fixed, if the rate rises you will usually be asked to make higher payments. If the rate falls, you have the option to reduce your payments. If you leave your payments unchanged when interest rates rise, the effect is to extend the term of the mortgage, possibly indefinitely; when rates fall, the effect is to reduce the term of your mortgage, if you continue making the same payments.

Some banks and building societies operate a system where they ask you to change your payments following interest rate changes at an annual review date. This means that for the time up to the annual review you are either repaying your loan more quickly or more slowly.

Tax relief

Most mortgages have basic rate tax relief granted at source. That means you pay less to the lender than you would otherwise. With a 25% basic rate of tax, this reduces a £100 interest payment to £75. Most mortgages have tax relief granted at source. For more about tax relief, see Chapter 12.

Which type of mortgage?

There are two main types of mortgage: repayment and endowment. To complicate matters, there are different types of repayment mortgages and different types of endowment mortgages. Which is preferable also depends on the interest rate at the outset, and whether in the future it is likely on average to remain at about the same level or to rise or fall substantially. It also depends on the performance of the endowment insurance policy. Unfortunately, over the twenty-five year term of a mortgage these are both factors which are very difficult to forecast.

Repayment mortgages

With a repayment mortgage you pay interest and also repay some of the capital each month. The amount of each combined payment depends on the rate of interest at the time and the initial term over which you have chosen to repay. The payment is fixed at the outset by the lender, but can vary in the future as rates of interest vary. You can get tax relief on the interest, but not on the capital.

There are two types of repayment mortgage: those with level payments and those with a low start and rising payments.

Level payments

This is the most common type of mortgage now available, and in fact the only one which many building societies offer. Your payments are worked out by the lender taking the rate of interest charged and knocking off the basic rate of tax. For example, if the mortgage rate was 10%, and the basic rate of tax 25%, then the lender would use a 7½% mortgage interest rate (that is, 10% less the 25% basic rate of tax) to work out your payments. Your mortgage payments would be a fixed level amount for the whole term of the mortgage (assuming interest rates remained unchanged).[1] Level payment mortgages are only available where the lender operates tax relief at source.

Varying payments (also called Gross Profile)

Your monthly payments are worked out first of all, ignoring tax relief. For example, the lender with a 10% mortgage rate uses 10% to work out the monthly mortgage payment. Part of this payment is interest, and part repayment of capital. Year by year as the capital is repaid the amount of interest in the payment is reduced and the capital repaid increases. So in each subsequent year of the mortgage the amount of interest paid is less. You only get tax relief on the interest, not on the repayment of capital. So although the before-tax-relief payments remain level (assuming interest rates do not change), the after-tax-relief payments rise year by year.

Where the lender operates tax relief at source, basic rate tax is deducted from the interest element of the payment, so you only have to make a payment after basic rate tax relief. However, as the tax relief reduces each year, so your payment rises each year (or each month with some banks).

Varying payments mortgages are available as an option at Barclays Bank, Halifax Building Society and Guardian Building Society. It is the only method of repayment mortgage at most other banks including Lloyds, Midland, National Westminster, Royal Bank of Scotland and TSB, and also at the National & Provincial Building Society.

Where tax relief at source is not operated by the lender, the monthly payments do not change (assuming interest rates do not), but the tax relief granted direct by the Inland Revenue falls year by year, which if deducted from the payments would show the same effect, i.e. rising payments after tax relief.

How long to repay

The longer the term may be, the lower are the payments, on either type of repayment mortgage. Generally mortgages are for terms of twenty-five years. If you want to have them repaid by the time you retire at sixty or sixty-five, you may choose a shorter term. Generally speaking, repayment mortgages of less than twenty years work out at a higher true rate of interest or APR. This is because of the way building societies and some banks (National Westminster and TSB) work out their payments. Mortgages of over twenty-five years have little attraction, as the extra term does little to reduce the payments.

Most building societies will let you increase your payments if you wish. This has the effect of reducing the mortgage term. The idea is that if later a wife stops work to have a baby, then at that point the mortgage term can be extended and the payments reduced. Choosing at the outset to pay more for a shorter term might be a good ploy if you expect the mortgage rate to rise and you do not want to pay more then. Check that your society will allow you to do this, as nowadays many require higher payments whenever the interest rate is raised.

Mortgage protection policies

It seems prudent to make sure that if you were to die, you have enough life insurance to pay off the mortgage. A special cheap policy called a mortgage protection policy is designed to do just this and automatically pays off whatever you owe if you die before you have finished repaying your mortgage. It is sensible to have such a policy with whichever of the two types of repayment mortgage you choose.

If you have a joint mortgage with both partners earning, it can be a good idea to take out a joint mortgage protection policy. This pays out if either of you dies – and is cheaper than taking two separate policies.

Premiums can be paid monthly or yearly. If you take out another form of life insurance, say a family income benefit policy, at the same time from the same company and pay the premiums together, you can usually get a discount. Mortgage protection policies can be obtained through building societies, insurance brokers, banks or direct from insurance companies. The Trustee Savings Banks include free life insurance for mortgages up to £50,000.

Always check the cost of the mortgage protection policies with two or three insurance companies, and be sceptical of the cost of a mortgage protection policy given on a quotation for an endowment mortgage. The companies trying to push endowment policies often have expensive mortgage protection policies, or make them look expensive by quoting policies where you do not pay premiums for the full twenty-five years, or policies which give more insurance than you need. By making the repayment mortgage look more costly, they make the endowment look cheaper.

Endowment mortgages

With an endowment mortgage you pay only interest on the loan. There is no repayment of capital, so your monthly payments to the lender are lower than with a repayment mortgage. However you must also pay premiums on an endowment life insurance policy which is large enough, when it matures, to pay off your loan. The lender takes the insurance policy as security as well as your home. The lender may be a bank, a building society or the insurance company itself. An endowment policy also pays off the loan if you die early – so there is no need for a mortgage protection policy as well.

There are six main types of endowment insurance policy which can be linked to an endowment mortgage. They are: lower cost with-profits, low start lower cost with-profits, full with-profits, unit-linked, pension, and non-profit endowment.

Lower cost with-profits endowment

A lower cost (or low cost) with-profits endowment policy is one specially designed for mortgages. A lower cost policy does not guarantee to pay off the loan on maturity of the policy. But the insurance company has worked out that, with the addition of profits over the years as bonuses, it will do – and also leave a little spare cash for you. What it does guarantee is that if you die before the policy matures, all the loan will be paid off. This is the most common type of endowment mortgage.

There are some seventy different lower cost policies to choose from. These are surveyed regularly in specialist magazines.[2] These surveys show the monthly premium and an estimate by the company of how it expects the policy to do in the future. Some show how well an ordinary with-profits policy did in the past.

Some of these policies, particularly if supplied through a large building society, do not require medical examinations, if the policy is taken out when you get a new mortgage. In that case, someone in poor health might get cheaper insurance than he or she otherwise would, or succeed in getting a policy which might have been refused. Most also give you the option to raise the amount of insurance if you want to get a larger mortgage later.

Low start lower cost with-profits endowment

This is the same as lower cost endowment, but the premiums are cheaper at the outset and rise during the first five or ten years.

Full with-profits endowment

As well as a guarantee to pay out a sum to repay your mortgage in full at the end of the term, or if you die earlier, a full with-profits policy also pays you profits. By the end of the term you expect these profits (added yearly or three yearly as bonuses to the sum insured) to increase to considerably more than the sum you will need to repay your loan.

The catch to this formula is that you have to pay high premiums for the endowment policy. A full with-profits policy is therefore an additional means of saving which you will normally not be able to afford in the early years of a mortgage.

Nowadays, a full with-profits endowment mortgage makes the burden of repaying a mortgage very heavy indeed in the early years. I would therefore not recommend it unless you already happen to have such a policy in existence. If you have, you should try to get a building society to agree to a part repayment and part endowment mortgage using your existing policy as security for the endowment part. This way you will have lower payments than with a full repayment mortgage.

Unit-linked mortgage

These work in a similar way to other endowments, except that you have an insurance policy which is linked to a unitised fund instead of 'with-profits'. It is impossible to predict whether this will be a better way to link an endowment mortgage than a lower cost endowment. It is worth considering if the premiums are lower and your lender accepts the policy.

Pension mortgage

A pension mortgage works in much the same way as a with-profits endowment mortgage, but instead of the endowment policy, you take out a Personal Pension (or a Retirement Annuity if you already had one before 1 July 1988).

The Personal Pension pays a lump sum at age 60 or later and this goes to pay off the mortgage. There is also a pension for the rest of your life. The reason a pension mortgage is attractive is because you get tax relief on the contributions at your highest rate; new endowment policies get no tax relief.

With a pension mortgage you also have to take out a term insurance policy to pay off the mortgage if you die early. This can also be eligible for full tax relief. You cannot take a mortgage linked to a Personal Pension if you belong to a job pension scheme.

Non-profit endowment

A non-profit endowment policy guarantees to pay out a sum exactly equal to the amount you need to repay your mortgage at the end of the term or if you die earlier; they are best avoided.

Finding the cheapest mortgage

At a mortgage interest rate of 7.5% to 8.5%, there is not a lot to choose between the different methods of repaying a mortgage. At higher rates than this, endowments become less attractive with the exception of the pension mortgage for those eligible.

The cheapest method when you start is undoubtedly a *varying payments repayment mortgage*. It will be the cheapest in the early years except when extremely low rates of interest are given, e.g. where you get a cheap loan, say 4%, from your employer.

Your next choice depends on whether you think interest rates are on average going to remain below 7.5% to 8.5% for the term of your mortgage or will on average be higher.

If you think interest rates will stay lower than 7.5% to 8.5%, then you should go for a *lower cost with-profits endowment mortgage*. This is also attractive to people who want to repay their mortgages over a shorter period of time than twenty-five years and those aged forty-five or more, who will find mortgage protection policies relatively more expensive. At interest rates of less than 8.5%, this is a cheap method; at 8.5% it can still be cheaper for some people than repayment mortgage with level payments.

If you think interest rates will be higher than 8.5%, and you can't get a varying payments repayment mortgage, you should choose a *level payments repayment mortgage* or a *lower cost endowment mortgage*. Different costs are given in Table 7.

Index-linked mortgages

With an index-linked mortgage you pay a lower rate of interest – say, 3%, 4% or 5% – but your payments are raised by reference to an index of prices. With this type of mortgage you should be able to borrow more to begin with, and payments can be lower at the outset. However, you may live to regret this in the future. As inflation has fallen, such mortgages have gone out of fashion because people willing to lend money linked to inflation have declined.

Ending your mortgage early

Many people move house well before the end of their mortgage term. If they have a repayment mortgage, they just pay off the amount outstanding with the proceeds of the sale and then can make a new choice of what sort of mortgage to have on their new home.

Where you have repaid the mortgage during the first five years or so you may be asked to pay a redemption charge. Sometimes this charge is waived if you give three months' notice or if you take out a new loan from the same society a short while afterwards. Most of the largest societies no longer make an early redemption charge. Some societies, however, charge interest until the end of the calendar month in which you repay. So if you repay on the 1st you can find yourself paying interest for one month longer than if you paid off a day earlier, e.g. the 31st of the month before.

If you had an endowment mortgage you must decide what to do with the policy. On moving house you are likely to be taking a larger

Table 7 Mortgage costs at 11¾% mortgage rate

Type	*Payments*	*Monthly for £20,000 mortgage*[1] £	*Monthly life insurance*[2] £	*Total monthly payment* £	*Payment in 25 yrs time*
Repayment mortgages Varying payments or Gross Profile	Rises each year	160 in yr 1	6	166	No
		162 in yr 5	6	168	
		165 in yr 10	6	171	
		172 in yr 15	6	178	
		183 in yr 20	6	189	
Level net payments	Level	167	6	173	No
Endowment mortgages					
Lower cost	Level	147	27	174	Modest amount
Lower cost low start	Insurance rises in first 5 yrs	147	17 in yr 1	164	Modest amount
		147	35 in yr 5	182	
Non-profit	Level	147	39	186	No
With-profits	Level	147	70	217	Large amount
Pension mortgage	Level	147	34[3]	181	Modest amount + pension

[1] After basic rate tax relief.
[2] Premiums for man aged 34.
[3] Includes personal pension contributions after tax relief at 25%.

mortgage and the endowment policy will not be large enough to cover the whole loan. If you take a new endowment policy to cover the difference, it will often be more expensive as the cost of life insurance policies increases with age.

You could ask the new lender whether it will allow you to have a part repayment, part endowment mortgage using your existing endowment policy to cover the endowment portion. The repayment portion could mature at the end of, say, twenty-five years even if the policy only has fifteen years more to run.

With an existing full with-profits policy the lender may be prepared to take into account some or all of the bonuses which have been added to the policy, as well as the basic sum insured.

If you are short of money, another alternative is to keep your endowment policy going completely separate from the mortgage, borrow extra against its security from the insurance company or your bank and take out a repayment mortgage.

Whatever you do, it is well worth keeping up a with-profits policy – what you get back on maturity is often worth a great deal more than if you surrender (i.e. cash it in early), even taking into account the extra premiums you have paid. And policies taken out before 14 March 1984 still get tax relief at 15% on the premiums (reducing to 12½% from 6 April 1989). But if you have a non-profit policy or a with-profits policy with a poor value company then cut your losses.

If you are considering paying off your mortgage because you have come into some money, first make sure you will have some money left over as an emergency fund after the mortgage is repaid. Also consider whether you might want borrow to buy something in the future; a new car, for instance. A mortgage with tax relief is likely to be the cheapest way you will ever be able to borrow. It is much better to keep the mortgage going and pay cash for future purchases, than to pay off the mortgage and then find you have to borrow again at a far greater cost.

Notes

1 See Appendix 2 for table of monthly repayments at different rates of interest and over different periods of time.

2 *Which?*; *Money Management*; *Planned Savings*.

7

Conveyancing and Solicitors

When people talk about the deeds of a house they usually mean the pile of legal documents which prove the ownership of a house. A conveyance is a deed which conveys a house from the vendor (the person selling) to the purchaser.

The legal process

In the UK, other than in Scotland where things are done differently (see p. 77), the purchase of a house is made in two stages. The first stage is up to when contracts are exchanged. This is the most important part. The contract is your written agreement to purchase the property and the vendor's agreement to sell it to you. Until contracts have been exchanged either buyer or seller can withdraw.

The contract describes what is being sold (e.g. the dwelling house known as 32 Hillview Gardens), the price to be paid and any extras or special conditions which have been agreed (e.g. to include carpets or lawn mower, or to repair the garden fence before leaving). It also gives the date when the deal will be completed – usually four weeks later. The contract includes a lot of standard conditions which describe amongst other things what happens if things go wrong. These standard conditions may be included by a clause referring to them even though they are not usually written into the contract (e.g. National Conditions of Sale Current Edition shall apply to this contract).

There are two identical copies of the contract and solicitors send draft contracts back and forth to each other with suggested amendments until you and the other party are agreed on all the points. If you are being granted a new lease then this is the time to agree all the points and clauses of the lease. If you are buying an existing lease you have to accept the lease as it stands.

When all these details have been hammered out, and also when your solicitor has completed his enquiries and searches (see below), you 'exchange' contracts. That is, you sign your copy of the contract, and the person you are buying from or selling to signs his copy. Then you exchange copies, the buyer paying a deposit – usually 10% – either to the seller's solicitor or, possibly, his estate agent.

Exchanging contracts really should be done simultaneously so that you do not end up obliged to sell without the purchaser being obliged to buy, and vice-versa. To enable this to be done, the purchaser's solicitor sends his contract, signed but undated, to the vendor's solicitor, and then (often by telephone) they agree the date to put in to make the transaction valid.

Between exchanging contracts and completion (i.e. the date when you are allowed to move in), your solicitor carries out some more investigations. He 'investigates the title'. This means he checks through the old conveyances going back at least fifteen years to make sure that the person selling actually owns the land. An 'abstract of title' is a summary of old conveyances. If the person selling has owned the house for more than fifteen years, then it is only the last conveyance which needs to be looked at. With registered property (see below) the solicitor has no deeds or conveyances to investigate; he merely sends a search form to the Land Registry for its certificate that no further entry has been made since the copy supplied by the vendor's solicitor before the contracts were exchanged. If it is leasehold, he checks the lease.

On completion, the balance of the price is exchanged for the deeds (including the transfer document signed by the vendor) and the keys: the purchaser then owns the house. After completion, any stamp duty is paid and the transfer, and mortgage, are registered at the Land Registry if applicable.

It often takes two to three months before you sign the contract and another month before completion. However, if you are unlucky to get caught in a chain of transactions in which one of the purchasers is delayed in obtaining a mortgage or whose deal falls through, you may end up waiting as long as nine months to a year before you finally move into your new home. If you are in a hurry there is usually no reason why contracts should not be exchanged within a week, or even a couple of days. Completion is usually four weeks after exchange of contracts, but could be as little as a week later if the searches and finance permit.

Registered and unregistered land

In England and Wales all land is either registered or unregistered. Since 1899 land registration has gradually been made compulsory over different areas of the country. Whether a property is already registered will depend on the area in which it is situated and how recently it was last sold. It is estimated that most private houses and flats are now within compulsory registration areas – so there is a good chance that the home you are buying is already registered – or, if not, will have to be registered after the transaction.

Once a property is registered in someone's name there is a State guarantee of ownership. The deeds and old conveyances can be dispensed with and are replaced by a Land Certificate which is a copy of the entry on the register kept at the local branch of the Land Registry.

Enquiries before contract

Before he advises you to sign a contract, the purchaser's solicitor sends the vendor's solicitor a list of questions about the house. Most of these are standard and most solicitors use a printed form with standard questions. Usually the answers are also in a standard form and part of the skill of a seller's solicitor is to conceal anything of importance (which might put somebody off buying) without making any false statements. This may mean the buyer does not get an answer to some questions – and other answers are such that you might as well have been given no reply. If you ask about the state of repair of the house for instance, the answer will almost certainly be something along the lines, 'The purchaser should rely on a survey'.

If there are any points which have not been fully answered and your solicitor thinks that the lack of response may be a clue to something amiss, he will probably seek clarification from the vendor's solicitor. He may also suggest you go and check whether some visible features of the property – like a right of way or a boundary fence – are actually where the deeds say they are. A solicitor rarely inspects a property himself – which is a good reason why you should go back and check that the documents match up with the house.

Local authority searches

This is a form with another set of standard questions which is sent to the local authority by the purchaser's solicitor and the replies obtained prior to signing the contract. Due to the rather ponderous procedure whereby your search has to be passed from department to department within the local authority, this can be a delaying factor in getting the contract exchanged. Your solicitor may get the search form back in a week or two – or it may take six to eight weeks. If there is any industrial action at the Town Hall you can be sure of long delays – fourteen weeks has been known.

If the local authority searches are expected to be clear, a contract can be signed subject to the searches being all right when they come. Solicitors are reluctant to advise clients to do this, just in case something unexpected crops up which may lead to a dispute as to whether the contract should be completed or not.

Where a previous deal has fallen through, it may be possible that the vendor can obtain recent searches from the purchaser who has let him down (he should offer to pay for them) and pass them on to the new purchaser. Replies to searches are usually taken as 'holding good' for two months.

The purpose of the local authority search is to bring to light amongst other things such important facts as whether a motorway is planned to pass through or near the property, or if the area is scheduled for slum clearance. The answers you get from local authorities are limited – they will not tell you about road improvements more than so many hundred metres from your boundary for example. And if you are new to an area it would be wise to make some additional personal enquiries at the Town Hall about local authority plans: reading the local newspapers regularly might also highlight something significant.

Land charges registry search

The land charges registry search paradoxically only applies to unregistered land and the purchaser's solicitor finds out from it whether the vendor is bankrupt or someone has registered a charge (other than a first mortgage) on the property, such as a second mortgage which the vendor has not disclosed. Again it is merely a matter of filling in a form, and mostly nothing of significance shows up. This type of search is made against the names of the owners of the property (past and present), not against the property itself. The Land Charges Registry for the whole country is at Plymouth.

Other things that solicitors do

The Law Society in its evidence to the Royal Commission on Legal Services[1] was asked to describe in chart form the steps necessary to complete various forms of conveyancing transaction. In the charts provided, a very noticeable feature is the amount of advice and help which solicitors are expected to provide which is not of a legal nature.

For instance solicitors may advise clients on the suitability of a survey (and always should do so); may instruct a surveyor for the client and obtain and often interpret the report for their clients; they may advise clients on finance, the mortgage offer, and whether or not they should take an endowment mortgage – all strictly non-legal and all matters which the client may or may not be better able to do himself.

A purchaser's solicitor may, at your request, negotiate with the vendor's solicitor over price and the state of repair of the property. He should ensure insurance cover is arranged from the date of the exchange of contracts (if a mortgage is involved the lender will probably do this automatically, but will need to know the date of exchange). It is the date of the contract, not completion, when the fire risk passes to the purchaser; in Scotland it is the date when the offer is accepted.

Of course in negotiations over price and so forth, your solicitor may merely be acting as a post-box for your instructions. Whether or not you think you could do better negotiating direct with the vendor or purchaser is up to you to decide. There is no law that says you have to communicate with the other side through your solicitor – although it is sensible to keep him informed of what you are doing, so that he does not do something inconsistent with your intentions.

Remember that whenever you have a solicitor acting for you, he should follow your instructions. You may ask for his advice and he may give you advice which you choose to ignore (sometimes at your peril), but if you ignore his advice you have only yourself to blame. On the other hand, you may think his advice is completely misguided – and if it is on a non-legal matter like the type of mortgage to take, or whether you think the survey report is to be relied on, then do not be afraid to have the courage of your convictions. If he strongly disagrees with you, it may be worth getting a second opinion from someone else.

Apportioning the rates

When you buy a house or flat you are liable to pay the rates and water rates from the day the purchase is completed. But as rates and water rates are generally paid half yearly in advance, the seller may already have paid for some of your rates unless you happen to buy your home early in the rate period, e.g. April or October.

On completion, the buyer refunds the seller the amount paid for any general and water rates for the period after completion, i.e. the rates are 'apportioned'. That means the buyer must pay a proportion of the rates and water rates bill which the seller has paid in advance. This amount is added to the purchase price on completion. The seller's solicitor works out the apportionment, and the buyer should check the calculations.

With telephone, gas and electricity supplies the utility company should normally give you a refund of any unused standing charges paid in advance. You should notify them of the completion date, and of your new address (see Chapter 11).

Choosing a solicitor

If you decide to use a solicitor to represent you and you do not already know one, ask your friends if they can recommend someone. Make sure that the recommendation is based on the solicitor having actually represented them, rather than being a casual golf club or bar acquaintance.

Even if recommended, ask the solicitor for an estimate of how much he will charge and compare it with some other estimates. Do not be fobbed off by the sort of answers which one newspaper reader reported in a survey.[2] 'I asked for an estimate beforehand but was told the fee would be kept as low as possible.' The Law Society provides a form for solicitors in England and Wales to give a written estimate of their charges and of other costs, so do not be afraid to ask for a written estimate if you are not offered one.

Solicitors are now allowed to advertise and it is well worth responding to an advertisement if you do not have a recommendation. Your solicitor need not be local to the house you are buying, although that might be useful in some circumstances.

The attitude of the person who answers the solicitor's telephone may be some guide to the efficiency with which he runs his office. In a small one- or two-partner firm it is possible that he or she may handle much of the conveyancing.

Remember to ask the solicitor whether he is on the panel of the building society where you hope to get your loan. If he is not, you will be lumbered with unnecessary extra expense. If you have difficulty finding a solicitor on the building society panel, ask your building society branch manager to recommend at least two, so you have a chance to compare estimates (see p. 35).

Unless you have been recommended someone in particular, I suggest you go for the cheapest – except of course if you know of someone who was not satisfied with the service obtained from him.

Doing your own conveyancing

The normal reason for doing your own conveyancing is to save money. However, I would not normally advise a first time buyer to contemplate a do-it-yourself job. With no previous experience of house purchase he is liable to be at a serious disadvantage when dealing with a building society, estate agents, the vendor and the vendor's solicitor. In any case, he will still have to pay the fees of a solicitor to act for the building society over the mortgage at a higher rate than would be charged if this solicitor was also acting for him. And he will not be saving any fees on a sale, so his scope for cutting costs is limited. On the other hand, a first time buyer only has to deal with the purchase, not a simultaneous sale. Doing one's first conveyancing transaction as a purchase only may be an easier training ground than attempting two transactions at the same time. Advice on how to keep a solicitor's conveyancing charges down is given in Chapter 4.

For someone who has experience of buying a house previously, doing the conveyance yourself can be a worthwhile way of saving money, especially if you are selling a house at the same time – you save both sets of legal fees. Some people think you should do your own conveyancing not only to save money but because you are likely to do a more thorough job. This would seem an unusual point of view – to insist that a layman can do a better job than the expert. But it is argued very convincingly by its chief advocate Michael Joseph in his book *The Conveyancing Fraud*.

Michael Joseph is a solicitor himself and spent fifteen years practising in conveyancing before he saw the light. His main thesis is that most conveyancing as practised by solicitors has developed into a ritual: often the steps in the transactions are not performed by solicitors but by their clerks (who may or may not be 'qualified' as members of the Institute of Legal Executives), and many if not all the really important points are left to chance. He reckons that what the layman lacks in experience he can make up in enthusiasm and by taking extra care: thoroughly inspecting the property himself and calling personally at the local authority instead of relying on standard forms of enquiry – with often meaningless or evasive answers to far too general questions.

Michael Joseph claims that conveyancing is neither complicated nor difficult. He says anyone capable of getting his own passport or road tax licence is capable not only of doing his own conveyancing but doing a far better job than a professional. But only you can judge whether you have the confidence and patience to undertake it yourself.

Buying a house takes time. If you are selling as well it takes even longer. You should not normally sign a contract to buy a new house until you are ready to sign a contract to sell your existing one. If you do, you may be left owning two houses – but with only enough money to pay for one. The same thing may happen to the person you are buying from. If somewhere along the line someone is unable to get fixed up with a mortgage, many other people's purchases and sales can be held up. This is called a mortgage-chain. One reason for using a solicitor is that he can sometimes use his influence to find a mortgage for someone further down the chain and thus get all the transactions rolling again.

Since writing the first edition of this book I have had a go at practising what Mr Joseph preaches, and did my own conveyancing on the purchase of a house. There was no mortgage involved, so I did not have the help of a building society solicitor. I found that the transaction was not quite as straightforward as the do-it-yourself manuals suggest, but on the other hand, they did cover every point which cropped up. From my experience, I think the best bit of advice I could give a do-it-yourself conveyancer is to assume you know at least as much as the solicitor on the other side; if what he says contradicts your manual, do not follow his advice, stick to the book. To do this you need to be a strongwilled and self-confident person, but if you are not you should not contemplate doing your own conveyancing. If you get a letter from the other side's solicitor which does not seem to make sense, do not hesitate to ask what he means. After all, you are not an expert. If you find a mistake, do not make a fuss about it – just make sure it is corrected. Bear in mind that there is nothing more annoying to any professional person than an amateur who is able to find him at fault.

However, there are a few instances where I would definitely advise against doing your own conveyancing: when you are buying a newly built house, when you are being granted a new lease or when you are buying a hitherto unregistered house in what is now a compulsory registration area. In the first two cases, snags on which you will require legal advice are likely to occur – and you will probably have to make the first registration which is usually more work than the registration of a transfer; in the latter case you definitely will have to make the first registration. In any event, people who do not have easy access to a typewriter and a photocopying machine will find do-it-yourself conveyancing very tedious. It is obviously essential, for example, to keep a copy of all your correspondence and of the documents.

There are two books I would recommend for someone contemplating do-it-yourself conveyancing: Michael Joseph's *The Conveyancing Fraud*, and Bradshaw's *Guide to DIY Buying, Selling and Conveyancing*. These are available through bookshops or direct from the publishers.[3] If you want to know more about conveyancing, even if you do not want to do it yourself, the books I have mentioned are worth reading.

Cut-price conveyancing organisations

There are a number of organisations which offer non-solicitor conveyancing services to the public. They are usually run by people who used to work in solicitors' offices as 'legal executives' or 'managing clerks' and who may be as experienced in the practical side of conveyancing as any solicitor. Their only advantage is that they can be cheaper than solicitors. They are now called Licensed Conveyancers.

The Law Society sets out the reasons why you should not go to a cut-price conveyancing organisation in a pamphlet.[4] It states: 'There are very few services that cannot be provided – by unqualified people – at a lower price than what is charged by those who do have a professional qualification. Those for whom price is the *only* consideration are the natural prey of the unqualified conveyancer.'

The pamphlet also lists a number of benefits of retaining solicitors, which it says do not apply to unqualified organisations. The most important of these in my opinion are that a solicitor must observe strict rules about keeping your money separate from his, he is covered by professional negligence insurance and the Law Society compensation fund (in case he runs off with your deposit) and he must never act for two people whose interests may conflict.

It would therefore be wise to enquire of a cut-price conveyancing organisation whether they are covered by professional indemnity insurance, for how much (£250,000 at least) and whether they are fidelity bonded (i.e. there is an insurance policy which will pay you if they run off with your money). Also ask for their most recent report and accounts, which should give you an idea of their scale of operations.

It might also be wise not to let any of your money actually be held by the conveyancing organisation. This may involve, if they act for the vendor, opening a special joint bank account to hold the deposit – and having to attend the completion personally to hand over or receive the purchase money.

Title insurance

A couple of cut-price conveyancing organisations offer Title Insurance as part of their service. This guarantees you against the insured loss if there should turn out to be a defect in your ownership and could help with the legal costs of a boundary dispute, for instance. It pays you compensation if you lose the case as well. Solicitors consider this insurance cover to be a gimmick and unnecessary and there seem to be very few claims. But if it costs you no extra, you might as well have it.

Scotland

One of the first things you will notice when contemplating buying a house in Scotland is that solicitors also act as estate agents. They are even allowed to call themselves 'Solicitor and Estate Agent'. As well as the normal methods used for buying and selling property in the rest of the UK (i.e. newspaper adverts, For Sale boards and circulars to interested parties) there are also Solicitors Property Centres.

At a Solicitors Property Centre you will find details of much of the local heritable property (the name Scottish lawyers use to describe property of the bricks and mortar variety). This is likely to provide a similar service to that of a rather large display in an estate agent's window. The difference is that it will have property on offer from all the solicitors in the area, so if there is no estate agent nearby you need go no further – except perhaps to look over the local newspaper for someone selling privately.

Only solicitors can advertise properties through Solicitors Property Centres although, of course, anyone can buy through them. Commission is charged by a solicitor for selling a house, in addition to his conveyancing fee.

Charges for conveyancing are what you agree with the solicitor. Always ask for an estimate, therefore, as you would elsewhere in the UK. Solicitors have forms on which they can give you a quotation spelling out all the charges.

If you are dissatisfied with a Scottish solicitor's charges you are entitled to have his bill submitted to 'taxation' by the Auditor of the Court of Session (even after you have paid it), but you will have to pay the cost of the taxation and the Auditor can raise the bill as well as lower it.

Dealing with offers

The major difference between English and Scottish land law is that in Scotland there is no such thing as an offer 'subject to contract'.

Any written offer you make can be binding on you – provided the other party chooses to accept it in writing. And the bargain can be concluded within twenty-four hours.

Although sales contracts, drafted and redrafted by the parties, are known in Scotland (as they are in the rest of the UK), they are uncommon and confined to complex business transactions.

Private house purchase is usually handled by a system known as 'missives of sale'; it is sometimes called blind bidding. A missive of sale is a written offer to buy a house in Scotland; it is binding on the person making it, but not on the seller until he or she accepts it.

Before you send the missive, you need to have your survey (and the building society valuation) made. The local authority enquiries are made by the vendor's solicitor – not by the purchaser's solicitor as elsewhere in the UK – so there will be no delay waiting for those.

Where there are several people competing for the same house, this is obviously a boon for local surveyors. Unfortunately there is little alternative as rarely will a seller agree to make a contract subject to a survey or the purchaser obtaining a mortgage. If a competing offer is accepted you have wasted the cost of your structural survey and building society valuation (which you have to pay for as you do elsewhere in the UK whether or not you take the loan). If you can find out (from the vendor) which surveyor has surveyed the property for another would-be purchaser, you might get him to do it again for you at a reduced fee.

Where there seems to be no competition for a home, it may be possible to make an offer subject to a satisfactory survey and loan offer. The contract becomes binding when these are received.

Preparing the missive is quite a skilled job. For instance, the seller may set a time limit by which he wants offers submitted. This will usually be the case where there is a lot of competition for the house. He will obviously want to sell to the highest bidder – which can be a bit perplexing at times of rapid house price inflation. If you are advised by your surveyor and solicitor that a house is worth £40,000 and to put in an offer of £38,000, it can be very disappointing if it goes to someone who offered £39,000 when you were ready to pay that amount if necessary. On the other hand, had you offered £42,000 you could remain blissfully ignorant that the next highest offer was only £35,000. Deciding on the price to offer when there are competing bidders is the most difficult part of the procedure in Scotland. The vendor's solicitor is not allowed to disclose what offers he has received – so all but one are bound to be disappointed. A local solicitor is usually the best source of advice on how much to offer.

Just as the seller may set a time limit by which he wants his offers in, you may often decide to put a time limit after which your offer lapses. If the property has been difficult to sell and you are making a low offer, then the time limit might be short to encourage acceptance rather than for the seller to hang on to see if a better offer will turn up. A seller may of course not accept your offer simply because he is waiting for his offer to purchase another house to be accepted. The Scottish system of binding missives means that the transaction is generally quicker than in England and Wales.

As well as the price offered and a description of the property, the missive will contain the 'date of entry', which is when you have to pay up and can move in. Convenient dates for both parties will usually have been discussed verbally – and of course an alternative date can always be agreed mutually.

There is no preliminary 10% deposit – the whole price is paid on 'settlement', the Scottish equivalent of 'completion'. Sometimes the price is paid in instalments – although according to the Law Society of Scotland a more satisfactory system is to treat the unpaid balance as a mortgage by the seller.[5]

Conveyancing

All property in Scotland is recorded in the Sasine Register, a property register established in 1617 and kept in Edinburgh. The Sasine Register also records mortgages and some other information and is open to public inspection. It differs from the English system of registered property because an entry in the Sasine Register does not guarantee that the deed registered there is valid (i.e. that the person who purports to own the property actually does so). Land registration similar to the English system is being introduced by districts.

Whereas in England for unregistered land a solicitor must look back at the title for fifteen years, in Scotland the period is ten years. Otherwise conveyancing is carried out by a system of deeds rather like the transfer of unregistered property in England and Wales.

You will find the Scots have their own legal jargon which is no easier (or more difficult) to understand than English legal jargon.

I know of no book on do-it-yourself conveyancing in Scotland. It would therefore be unwise to attempt a transaction on this basis without a guide on what to do.

Northern Ireland

The system of property transfer in Northern Ireland is broadly similar to that in England and Wales, although contracts are often signed speedily subject to a buyer obtaining a mortgage within a specified period and local authority enquiries being made and found satisfactory. A deposit of 10% is paid on exchange of contracts and is usually held by the seller's solicitor. It is returnable if the conditions of the contract are not met.

The organisation for solicitors in Northern Ireland is the Incorporated Law Society of Northern Ireland. You may find some aspects puzzling if you do your own conveyancing, as the do-it-yourself guides do not explain the differences between English and Northern Ireland practices.

Forms of ownership

Where you are buying a property jointly (with your husband or wife for example), there are two legal ways in which a property may be held. These are 'joint tenancy' and 'tenancy in common'.

Provided both owners remain living in the house there is no practical difference. With a joint tenancy, if the husband dies first, say, the house automatically passes to his wife, irrespective of what he puts in his will. This is not the case with a tenancy in common, where the husband's share would become part of his estate and pass according to the provisions of his will. The position is exactly the same if the wife dies first.

For many years solicitors automatically made joint purchases by a husband and wife into joint tenancies. This was because there was often an Estate Duty advantage by doing so. Nowadays, since the advent of Inheritance Tax, there is less advantage – and there could be an advantage in having a tenancy in common if you own a high value home jointly with someone who is not your husband or wife.

A joint tenancy can be severed by either party giving notice to the other. In such a case the ownership becomes a tenancy in common. If you particularly want to leave your half of the house to someone other than the person who owns the other half, then you should ensure that you have a tenancy in common. A solicitor is the best person to go to for advice on this matter.

Notes

1 Memorandum No. 3: Replies by the Council of the Law Society to the request for evidence from the Law Society by the Royal Commission, 1977.
2 *Daily Mail*, 14 September 1977.
3 For addresses see Appendix 3.
4 *Buying and Selling Your Home: Questions and Answers about Conveyancing*, Law Society.
5 Replies by the Law Society of Scotland to the Royal Commission on Legal Services in Scotland, Volume 1, October 1977.

8

Household Insurance

Your home is likely to be the most valuable asset you ever own. It is therefore essential that it is insured. Most likely you have also spent your remaining savings on furnishing it as nicely as possible, so the same should surely apply to the contents.

Having pronounced in favour of insurance, you should be under no illusion that insurance can compensate you for every piece of bad luck which befalls you. In fact the cynical would say that many an insurance policy seems to exclude all but the most rare occurrences.

Household insurance policies do not cover everything. You insure against certain named 'perils' like fire, flood and theft. If you incur a loss or damage to your property as a result of these perils the insurance company pays out, provided you have kept your insurance cover up to the right amount.

With items which depreciate in value, in the past you were never paid enough to replace the stolen or destroyed items as new. Your claim value was worked out according to the principle of 'indemnity'. Such a claim was calculated by deducting an appropriate proportion from the current replacement cost. One way of assessing this is to work out the useful life of an item; for instance if it were fifteen years for a three piece suite, they might knock off one-third from the replacement cost for a five-year-old suite.

Rather than haggling with an insurance company over a claim, it is better to put all your household insurance on a 'new-for-old' basis. You pay higher premiums but there should be no dispute about replacement costs – it will be the cost of replacement by a new item (except usually for clothing and bed linen). Choose from insurance companies which belong to the Insurance

Ombudsman Bureau, which will judge your case in the event of a dispute.

Household insurance policies are usually divided into two parts – buildings and contents. Insurance companies issue package policies containing both, but many people insure their buildings through one company and their contents through another.

Combined buildings and contents policies

A number of building societies have started selling combined buildings and contents policies. The insurance rate is based on the value of the house for rebuilding and the insurance automatically covers the contents. You should go for this type of policy if the 'combined' premium costs less than the total for two separate policies; this will depend on which area of the country you live in and how cheaply you can get your contents insured.

Even if you do not have a combined policy, it may be more convenient to have both buildings and contents insurance policies with the same company; then there will be no argument about which company should pay.

Buildings insurance

People buying a home with a mortgage are usually obliged to insure the buildings with an insurance company chosen by the lender. Building societies should give you a choice of at least three companies and possibly a choice of premiums for different types of cover. But if your house is liable to a higher than average premium – say four to eight times for a thatched cottage – it is well worth shopping around yourself and trying to persuade the building society to use a cheaper company or let you take out your own insurance. Some building societies make a charge for this. For thatched and timber buildings consider these specialist brokers: Burgoyne Alford, CGA (Insurance Brokers), or Thatchowners (Insurance Agency).

Inclusions and exclusions

The policy normally covers damage caused by fire, earthquake, lightning, explosion, storm, flood, water escaping from pipes or tanks, impact of aircraft, rail and road vehicles or animals, falling trees, theft or attempted theft, breakage of aerials, oil leaking from central heating installations, riot or malicious damage (but not in Northern Ireland) and subsidence, landslip and usually heave (the opposite of subsidence).

In the case of subsidence or landslip you normally have to pay the first 3% of the total rebuilding cost of your house, or the first £250, whichever is the higher. For a £40,000 house this means you pay the first £1,200 of any subsidence or landslip claim. However, with some policies issued through building societies, the clause states 'whichever is the lower', in which case you would only pay the first £250 or whatever other sum is specified.

In the case of escaping water, impact by a vehicle driven by you or a member of your family living with you, or damage as a result of riot, malicious damage or falling trees, the first £15 is often not covered. You can usually pay an extra premium to have this £15 'excess' deleted. However, it is not really worthwhile deleting such small excesses. The subsidence excess cannot be deleted.

If the damage is so bad that you have to live elsewhere until it is repaired, then the insurance will often pay the cost of alternative accommodation, up to a maximum of 10% of what the building is insured for.

In addition to the structure, a buildings policy covers interior decorations; built-in furniture; bathroom fittings; plumbing and central heating (but not repairs to the piping); greenhouses, tool-sheds; fences and garden walls; drives; gates; and even swimming pools. Breakage of glass in windows or doors and bathroom fittings may also be covered – whatever the cause of damage.

Common exclusions are frost damage, storm or flood damage to gates and fences, escaping water damage if the house is left partially furnished or unfurnished for more than thirty days, and damage caused by war, civil war, rebellion or revolution.

Apart from the exclusions in the policy, insurance companies may refuse to pay out on a claim for some other reasons – when what they call a 'material fact' has not been disclosed by you. Insurance companies have agreed with the Government[1] that they should ask you direct questions about material facts (and if they do not, you should disclose them).

These material facts include whether the house is used for a business (even part time); whether you leave the home unattended regularly during the daytime; whether you take lodgers; whether it is in an area subject to flood, subsidence or landslip; whether it is in good repair; whether in the past three years there has been an occurrence of any of the risks which are to be insured; whether the house is built of material other than brick, stone or concrete, and roofed with anything apart from tiles, metal, asphalt or concrete, and whether it is a holiday home or otherwise left empty for long periods. If any of these apply, you can expect to pay higher premiums or have your cover restricted. Some insurance companies offer 'all risks' buildings insurance which covers any accidental damage, like putting your foot through a ceiling.

Blocks of flats

In the case of a flat there is usually one buildings insurance policy for the whole block. Each tenant pays his share of the premium, but normally has no say in the choice of insurance company – the landlord is obliged, under the terms of the lease, to make sure that the insurance is adequate.

Where the landlord is careless or incompetent, there can be serious gaps in the insurance of a flat – possibly through underinsurance. Some insurance brokers offer an insurance policy designed to top up a landlord's cover.[2]

When you buy a flat, you, or your solicitor, should ask the landlord to inform the insurance company of your right to a share of the insurance proceeds by 'endorsing your interest on the policy'. If you buy your home on a mortgage, the lender will do this on its own behalf too.

How much to insure for

What you pay for your house is not necessarily how much you should insure it for. When you buy with a mortgage, the lender's valuer should make an insurance valuation, which is the amount for which the lender will insure it. Nowadays, most building societies insist on policies where the amount insured and premiums are linked to an index of building costs. This way you ensure that the insurance value does not fall behind because of inflation. If your policy is not index-linked, you should update the insured value every year.

Table 8 Examples of house prices compared with insurance values

	Market price £	*Estimated insured value* £
Non basement 2 bedroom terraced pre-1920		
Nottingham	19,000–25,000	63,000–76,700
Liverpool	12,000–22,000	66,500–83,000
Brighton	74,000–85,000	74,100–92,300
Semi-detached 3 bedroom 1930s		
Leeds	35,000–65,000	51,300–63,000
Oxford	80,000–100,000	60,800–74,100
Edinburgh	55,000–65,000	54,900–66,500
Bromley	92,500–140,000	66,700–81,000
Detached 4 bedroom – modern		
Norwich	85,000–140,000	55,400–98,100
Manchester	75,000–145,000	55,400–98,100
Ealing	188,000–250,000	67,800–120,300

Source: Prices from Woolwich House Price Guide July 1988. Estimated insured values based on Association of British Insurers recommended figures at September 1987, updated to June 1988.

The Association of British Insurers has a guide to rebuilding costs which it revises once a year. For more details you can get a free leaflet.[3] Rebuilding costs depend on the size of the house; when it was built; whether it is a 'semi', detached, terraced or a bungalow; and how much rebuilding costs are in the region in which it is situated. For details of how this varies by region see Table 8.

The cost of a buildings policy is £12 to £18 for each £10,000 worth of insurance (£16 is common). If your house is of non-standard construction you can pay from half as much again to eight times more.

Contents insurance

'Contents' comprise furniture, household goods and appliances (e.g. washing machine, cooker, fridge, television, hi-fi), clothing, moveable fixtures and fittings, furnishings (like carpets and curtains), food, drink; and valuables such as jewellery and money up to specified limits. Internal decorations come under the buildings policy – but may be covered under the contents in certain cases (e.g. a leasehold flat).

Single items are usually limited to 5%, sometimes 10%, of the total value you are insured for – unless you specify them to the insurance company. Usually not more than a third of the value must consist of valuables – defined as jewellery, gold and silver, furs, and so on. Some companies have a wider definition, including pictures, all antiques, cameras, etc. Theft is usually excluded when the home is let, sublet, or lent, unless there is evidence of forcible entry.

The insured 'perils' are the same as under the buildings policy, but if you are insured with a different company for buildings than for contents, you may have slightly different cover.

All risks cover

A contents policy does not usually cover your contents outside your house (sometimes outside your garden) except when you are moving house. Nor does it usually cover accidental damage except to specific items – an owned or rented television set is the main example.

Some home contents policies offer cover for accidental damage caused by your family's own clumsiness. While you may be able to claim for damage caused by burning a hole through a new sofa with a cigarette (because fire is a hazard against which you are insured), you will not be able to claim if you break the family Chinese vase collection unless your contents policy is of the 'all risks' variety. Usually the first £5 or so is excluded from these policies and there are exceptions for wear and tear, vermin, mildew and mechanical breakdown. The snag is that the cost is much greater.

Alternatively, you can have specific all risks extensions to a traditional contents policy for single valuable items. A valuable engagement ring, camera or fur which is frequently taken out of the house will need to be specified and an extra premium paid. The rate for this sort of all risks insurance varies very widely but you can expect to pay from four to ten times the premium for the same amount of cover as for your household contents. You can also get extensions for the contents of a freezer and your personal effects outside the home.

Money

Money (including credit cards, postage stamps, postal orders and season tickets) is covered under an ordinary contents policy but there is generally a £100 limit on a claim. Nor will the company pay for theft unless there is evidence of a forcible and violent entry. Should someone walk through the open front door and pinch your handbag, the bag would be covered, but not the money in it. However, for an extra premium you can also insure money outside the house up to £200, which would cover you for a walk-in theft.

New-for-old

In the event of a claim on a contents policy, you are likely to be much more satisfied if you have a 'new-for-old' or 'replacement-as-new' policy. This means that you are given the money to buy a new item even though the one destroyed or damaged beyond repair has depreciated in value since you bought it. But wear and tear on clothing and linen is still taken into account. The alternative is an 'indemnity' policy where wear and tear is taken into account on all items.

Some companies issue hybrid policies which are new-for-old during the first three or five years of the life of a large item (e.g. carpets, furniture) and indemnity thereafter; as well as indemnity for everything else.

I would strongly recommend a new-for-old policy. Having a new-for-old policy does mean that you should have a higher insured value than if you had an indemnity policy. But it is quite simple to work out – you just go round the shops totting up the prices of buying everything you have brand new. The easiest way is to make a list room by room.[4]

The cost of contents and all risks cover

Whilst buildings insurance often costs £15 or £16 for each £10,000 of insurance anywhere in the country, the cost of contents cover varies widely and is related to the varying incidence of theft in different parts of the country – and even different areas in the same town.

The cheapest will be around £25 to £30 for each £10,000 of insurance – although of course your contents are unlikely to be as valuable as your home so the actual premium you pay may be less.

The most expensive charge is around £150 for each £10,000 of insurance.

Contents insurance is particularly expensive in all London postal districts (especially North-West London and the West End), and the nearby areas of Edgware, Stanmore and Harrow. The next most expensive areas are the rest of Greater London, the outer London suburbs, Liverpool and Glasgow. If you have been with the same company for a long time they may not have increased your rate to what they would charge a newcomer.

All risks insurance for individual items outside the house is even more expensive. The premium would be from 1% to 3½%, say £10 to £35 a year for a £1,000 fur coat.

If you live in one of the areas I have mentioned above, it is worth getting quotes from more than one insurance company, as not all have the same rates for the same areas. You may have to pay higher rates if you live in a flat. Installing window locks and good door locks might help to keep your premium down, or may even be required before a company will accept you in a high risk area.

New policies are often index-linked – so the insured value and premiums are automatically increased. If you buy extra furniture, make sure you increase your insurance cover.

Legal liability

This is usually included with both buildings and contents policies. It covers you for your liability as a houseowner (buildings) or as an occupier (contents) if you are sued, for example, for accidents for which you are legally responsible. Normally there is a limit of £500,000 or £1 million on such claims.

Legal expenses insurance

A legal expenses insurance policy covers your legal costs if you get involved in a legal action. If you lose, it pays any costs awarded against you (but not damages).

Although there may be some serious exclusions (e.g. no claims against builders you have employed or against insurance companies) this can be a very helpful form of insurance for someone who at some time in the future is likely to get into a dispute and need legal advice which he may not be able to afford. Several companies offer legal expenses insurance. The cost is about £70 a year for a domestic household policy; but you can get an 'add-on' to your existing contents policy from insurance brokers for as little as £5 or £10 a year.

The sort of disputes these policies cover are those with traders such as shopkeepers, cleaners, garages and travel agents, and also disputes with neighbours, employers and public authorities. There is a special policy for people who want to rent out their home temporarily.

Notes

1 *Statement of Insurance Practice*, Association of British Insurers.
2 For example Chambers and Newman Insurance Brokers, see Appendix 3.
3 *A Guide to Buildings Insurance for the Homeowner*, Association of British Insurers.
4 See also the free leaflet *A Guide to Home Contents Insurance*, Association of British Insurers.

9

Living in Your Home

Having overcome all the hurdles of dealing with estate agents, building societies, surveyors, solicitors, insurance companies and well meaning relatives – all of whom seem to have been sent to try you – you may now be ready to live happily ever after in your new home. And most people do.

However, a major difference between an owner-occupier and a tenant is that an owner-occupier must make his own decisions. He cannot leave everything to the landlord – and he has no one but himself to blame if things do not go as planned. So this chapter is aimed at giving you a few hints on how to live happily in your home.

Rates, rateable value and community charge

Probably the first bill to come in will be the rates. This is a property tax collected by the local council. You may not have had to pay rates as a tenant – they may have been included in your rent.

Rates are based on the rateable value of your home. The rateable value is supposed to represent the rent at which your home could be let to a tenant after deduction of a fixed scale for maintenance. In practice the rateable value is no more than an arbitrary value put on your home.

Your rateable value may be increased if you make significant improvements to your home (e.g. an extension) and the council gets to know. Building a garage would also raise your rateable value.

You can appeal against your rateable value – for instance if your amenities are affected by a kennels opening up next door or a school or factory being built next to your back garden.[1] People who appeal against their rates need to have a lot of time on their hands. You are likely to achieve a small reduction (assuming you succeed, which you may not) in relation to the amount of work and effort put in. I do not recommend it.

When a home is empty and unfurnished, no rates are payable for the first three months. After that period the local council has discretion about any reduction it gives.

Community charge

From April 1990 (April 1989 in Scotland) the Government proposes to replace domestic rates with a new tax called the community charge. This tax does not depend on the rateable value, but is a fixed amount which each person over age 18 who lives permanently in the household is liable for. The amount of the charge will vary according to which local authority area you live in. But it will be the same whatever the size or age or value of your home. The community charge is usually called the 'poll tax' but it has nothing to do with your right to vote and not paying it does not disenfranchise you. The community charge will benefit single ratepayers and single parents who will generally pay less than they did with rates. It will also benefit people with homes with high rateable values. Losers will be young adults living with their parents who previously did not have to pay the rates but will have to pay the community charge.

Paying the rates or community charge

You pay the rates or community charge to the Finance Department of your local council. The bill often comes in two instalments – in April and October. You can either pay it by the time stated on the demand or you have the right to pay by ten or more equal instalments starting in April and ending in January – so you have nothing to pay in February and March; it is most convenient to arrange a standing order at your bank for these. Most people pay by instalments. You can be prosecuted and imprisoned for not paying the rates or community charge.

Rebates

There are also rebates whereby you may be able to get a reduction or rebate on your rates or community charge if your income is low in relation to the rates you pay.

You cannot get one if your savings or investments, excluding the value of your home, are more than £8,000.

The rebates are higher for families with children and for one-parent families; they are lower if your children are in regular employment. There is also a special extra rebate for severely disabled people.

Water, gas, electricity, fuel, telephone

Water rates cover the cost of sewage disposal as well as the provision of water. You can usually pay the water rates in two, four or ten instalments. You cannot get a rebate on the water rate. As the water rate is based on the rateable value of your home, your bill does not depend on your water consumption, although the basis for assessing water charges is likely to change after 1990 when ordinary rates are abolished.

Gas and electricity bills are sent quarterly and, depending on your method of heating, the winter ones are likely to be much heavier than the summer ones. All gas and electricity boards give you the chance to pay monthly at no extra charge. They use your last year's bills to estimate what next year's will be, and divide by twelve to get the monthly payment. At the end of the year you make an adjustment for what you have under- or overpaid. Oil and coal bills can often be spread out in monthly payments – but you may get a discount by paying all at once. Alternatively you may be able to pay these bills by credit card. Telephone bills are quarterly, and can be paid monthly.

Other bills

Other expenditure is unlikely to be as readily spread. Life insurance premiums can usually be paid monthly rather than annually. Some companies let you pay car insurance in five or six instalments at no extra cost. You can pay your building insurance to the building society by adding one twelfth of the annual premium to your monthly mortgage payments, and the same applies to the contents insurance if you have insured through the building society. Season tickets can sometimes be financed by interest free loans from your employer – ask if he has a scheme. A ground rent and service charge on a flat might be spread to quarterly payments instead of half yearly.

If there are still too many lump sum bills, you could ask your bank if it runs a budget account, but you have to pay a charge and interest for such a facility, unlike most of the methods described above which are free.

Service charges

If you own a flat, your lease is likely to stipulate that the cost of common services is shared between all the tenants. So, in addition to your ground rent, you get a bill for your share of cleaning the communal halls, maintaining any garden, for any repairs and decorations which are carried out, and for the insurance.

Normally the ground landlord or his agent makes an estimate of the expenditure in advance and you make payments of an 'advance service charge' towards the cost. Once a year you should be sent accounts or receipts showing the total expenditure, and you then have to pay any extra (there never seems to be a refund although there could be).

Large blocks of flats may have a sinking fund to provide for the cost of future large-scale works. This means the money is saved up for three or four years in order to lessen the amount you have to pay when the work is carried out. Unfortunately sinking funds do not work well when inflation is high as they cannot do much to cut the eventual bill.

When expenditure of over £500 is proposed on a single item a landlord must obtain two estimates and let the tenants have the opportunity of seeing and commenting on them at least a month in advance.[2] The freehold of some blocks of flats is owned by a management company which in turn is owned by the residents themselves. So in practice it is the residents' association which is the landlord. Even where this is not so, a well run residents' association, especially in a large block, can negotiate with the landlord's agents and make life for the residents happier.[3]

Heating

One of the most expensive costs of running a home is heating. In this era of so-called energy shortage, saving fuel is now what the government wants everyone to do. *Which?* magazine makes periodic surveys of the costs of different forms of heating. Insulating the loft and lagging your hot water tank are the cheapest ways of saving on heating costs. Details of this and other methods can be found in leaflets published by the Department of Energy and the Department of Environment. You can even get a grant from your local council to insulate a loft, hot and cold water tanks and pipes for the first time or to bring loft insulation up to a modern standard if your house was built before 1976 and you are on a low income.[4]

Double glazing, which is expensive, is not recommended as a method of insulating a home against heat loss, although it may be useful against noise. Cavity wall insulation, also expensive, may be worth having if your house is of suitable construction. There are a number of trade associations which can give advice on these matters, such as the Glass and Glazing Federation and the National Cavity Insulation Association.[5]

If you have not already got central heating, you may think it well worth while to install it. At the time of writing, gas is the cheapest fuel for central heating. However, in the two years 1985 to 1987, the cost of central heating oil halved.

Gas is more convenient in that there is rarely a shortage of supplies (e.g. through a tanker drivers' strike) and you do not need space for a storage tank. However, in some country areas gas is not available. A source of information on this is the Heating and Ventilation Contractors' Association, and for gas installers there is CORGI.[5]

Alternatively you might consider solid fuel, although this will have to be a special smokeless type – no log fires – if you are in a smokeless zone. Your solicitor's local authority enquiries will give the answer to that. For more details there is a leaflet.[6]

Maintaining your home

Decorations

You will probably want to decorate your new home inside as soon as you move in, and you will probably want to do it yourself. There are a number of extremely useful books on do-it-yourself which tell you how to paint, hang wallpaper and put up tiles, and also all about almost any household repair or improvement you are likely to want to carry out yourself.

Inside decorations can last quite a long time – so if you do not expect to stay in the same house for more than seven years or so, you will not have to bother to redecorate once you have done it initially. Outside decorations, however, have to be done more frequently – every four years is the usual interval. If you leave it for five years the paint is likely to be peeling off the window frames. You might want to do it every three years if your house is particularly exposed to harsh weather conditions.

If you are making any structural alterations (e.g. rewiring, installing central heating, or replacing the bathroom) it is obviously sensible to try and time this to take place shortly before you are due to have decorations done. Otherwise you will have to spend extra time touching up the inevitable damage to decorations caused by such installations.

Should you decide to have the decorations done for you – either inside or out – you should ask at least two, preferably three, decorators to give you a quote. Specify in detail what you want done – e.g. two coats of oil paint, garage doors to be stripped to wood, inside of bedroom fitted cupboards included in painting. You could even give a written specification, perhaps amending it in the light of a decorator's comments as he looks round the house.

Large firms and some small ones will give you a written quote. One-man-bands may not. Occasionally you get someone calling who is only acting as an agent for other contractors and will not be doing or supervising the work himself. With a small firm, it is always worth asking whether the man you see will be doing or supervising the work.

The quotes you get can often vary enormously. One year I got three contractors to estimate for painting the outside of my house. The quotes were £250, £350 and £1,200, and with the cheapest quote I was to supply my own paint which cost £100. I chose the cheapest.

With smaller contractors, one way of keeping the price down, especially where there is a lot of painting, is to get a quote including materials – and then ask how much less it would be if you supplied your own. My experience has been that painters often vastly overestimate the amount of paint needed. They often buy from a trade supplier who may charge more than what you might pay at a do-it-yourself cash and carry. In another instance I was quoted ten gallons of paint at a cost of £9 a gallon. In the end he used six gallons which I bought for £6 a gallon. (Paint costs rather more today!)

Plumbers, electricians, carpenters, roof repairs

Decorating is a relatively unskilled but time-consuming job carried out at lengthy intervals. However, if something goes wrong with the plumbing or you want an alteration made to the position of a power point, or you want to have a fitted cupboard made or the roof starts to leak, your choice of contractor is more difficult. Taking the cheapest will rarely be the best alternative.

By their nature, poorly done decorations show up and can usually be remedied easily; if a poorly painted window starts peeling, it does not take much to touch it up on a Sunday morning. This is not the case with other sorts of poor workmanship. If a pipe starts leaking as a result of a plumber doing a bad job you have to get him (or another plumber) back immediately to remedy the damage.

So go on recommendation first and price second for such jobs. If you have no recommendation then you will have to get quotes from more than one contractor, except, of course, in cases of emergency. Nevertheless even in an emergency, or if you are only considering one man, always ask for an estimate of the cost unless the job is only a small one and you are pretty sure of his general level of charges from a previous job.[7]

Local newspapers are often a source of advertisements for tradesmen. Often good tradesmen are in such demand that you have to wait a very long time for them to come and do the job. There are registration schemes for gas and electrical installers and you can get a list of local registered tradesmen.[8] Installations are best done by people registered with the respective councils.

Noise

You may live in the idyllic countryside but you are more likely to live in a town or suburb. The best way of avoiding noise is not to buy a home affected by it. But the noise may arrive after you move in – or you did not know about it. Information on what to do about noise and how in some circumstances you can get insulation grants are given in two leaflets.[9]

Disputes with neighbours

Disputes with neighbours can make life very difficult – and the fact that you may meet almost daily makes such a dispute one of the most bitter.

Boundaries are the most common cause of a serious dispute. One neighbour building a fence or wall only a foot (and sometimes less) on the wrong side of a boundary can start all manner of fuss.

Trees are probably the next most common cause. If you own the tree and it causes you damage, you promptly cut it down. But if it is your neighbour who complains of the tree casting shadows over his patio, choking his drains with leaves, breaking his plants with falling branches or undermining his foundations with its roots, it is amazing how essential you may feel the tree is to the leafy environment of the street! You might even get the council to put a preservation order on it.

Other causes of annoyance are children and animals. Large dogs can terrify small children; and medium sized children can terrify elderly widows – often not by what they do, but what the neighbour thinks they may do. Disputes over shared driveways, rights of way, and even the positioning of garden lights have been known.

There is rarely a satisfactory solution once a dispute gets going until one or other of the neighbours moves away. Arguing over the fence usually makes things worse, and getting a solicitor to obtain an injunction against a neighbour to stop his doing something is rarely worth the trouble or expense.

The best approach is undoubtedly a good neighbour policy. Whenever you see your neighbours, exchange a cheery word, pat their dog, comment (favourably) on their children, offer them the occasional plant from the garden, and sometimes do them a small favour. If you have been looking after next door's dog for a week while they are on holiday and you reverse your car straight through their garden wall ruining their favourite flower bed, you are likely to be able to weather the storm far better than if you had never done them a favour. Incidentally, that example is a true one – though I hasten to add I was neither car driver nor dog owner.

Lend your step ladder. Look after a spare set of keys. Invite your neighbours in for tea or a drink at Christmas. These are all ways of building up neighbourliness which will lessen the impact of a dispute if it subsequently occurs.

If you fall into dispute and do not want a fight, then the best thing to do is to give in or move elsewhere. If you do not mind a fight you would cut the costs if you had legal expenses insurance (see Chapter 8).

Securing your home

Professional burglars will probably boast that they can get into any home if they put their minds to it. But the more difficult you make it for them, the less likely they are to try. You should also remember that not all thieves are so expert. An increasing number of children are involved in domestic break-ins and some may be put off by the simplest precautions. Surprisingly enough, it is still mainly a matter of locks and bolts. Make sure that all the outside doors to your home have mortice locks on them – and that when you go out, even for ten minutes, you lock them. You may be surprised how little time a thief needs to stay in your home. There is no point in locking inside doors; burglars are then likely to smash them, causing you even more aggravation. Closing inside doors unlocked is a useful fire precaution, however.

You can get free advice on what type of locks – and whether you need anything more elaborate – from the Crime Prevention Officer at your local Police Station. The advantage of consulting him – apart from the fact that he has no axe to grind for one particular form of protection – is that he knows what sort of crime is prevalent in your area and what sort of villain is likely to be attracted to your home.

Happily, most thieves do not want to break into your home while you are there. So if you can make them think you are home when you are not, so much the better. This means leaving on all the lights you normally put on during a winter afternoon. Leaving the hall and lavatory lights on is almost as good as leaving the thief a note that you are out.

Outside lights illuminating your garden and walls are likely to discourage people shinning up drain pipes. You can buy adaptors which turn lights on and off in the house at random, or time and light sensitive switches which turn off and on at set times or when it gets dark. Putting a radio on one of these time switches is also a useful deterrent.

You can also paint your drainpipes with special paint which never dries and stops people climbing up.

In spite of taking all possible precautions you may still be burgled. If you want to help catch the thief or have a chance of getting your goods back, take photographs beforehand of valuable ornaments or jewellery and keep a note of the serial numbers of television sets, radios, hi-fi equipment, cameras and so on. It will also help with your insurance claim.

Notes

1 It is the Inland Revenue Valuation Office or District Valuer, probably situated at your Town Hall or local council offices, who is responsible for working out rateable values.

2 Where there are over twenty flats the limit is £25 per flat. There is a free leaflet *Service Charges in Flats*, Department of Environment, Welsh Office.

3 For advice on setting up and running a residents' association, join the Federation of Private Residents' Associations.

4 See leaflet *Save money on loft insulation*, Department of Environment.

5 For addresses see Appendix 3.

6 *Smoke is our Enemy*, Department of Environment.

7 Advice on tackling tricky maintenance jobs can be obtained from Building Research Service publications. For addresses see Appendix 3.

8 National Inspection Council for Electrical Installation Contracting (NICEIC) and Confederation for the Registration of Gas Installers (CORGI).

9 *Bothered by Noise*, Noise Advisory Council; *Land Compensation, Your Rights Explained; No. 5 Insulation against traffic noise*; Department of Environment.

10

Thinking Ahead

This chapter concerns planning for the future while you remain in your present home. It includes improvements and extensions, using your home to get better holidays and where to look for help if you fall on hard times.

Improving or extending your home

Most people make minor adaptations and alterations to their home. But if you live in a house and have the space you might think it worth while extending or altering your home in a more major respect.[1] Alternatively you may have bought a dilapidated house with the express purpose of improving it. The most popular extensions are adding a utility room, extending an existing kitchen, installing an additional wc and adding an extra bedroom. Consider carefully whether the improvement will increase the value of your house when you want to sell. Central heating will probably pay for itself in full, as might an extra bedroom or a garage; but an extra reception room might not.

For improvement work generally, it is worth asking your lender if the expense can be met by increasing your mortgage. A bank or other loan for home improvement purposes does not qualify for tax relief on the interest payments (see Chapter 12).

Home improvement grants

Grants are available from local councils for the improvement (and sometimes repair) of houses built before 1961 (in Scotland 1964). They pay a proportion up to 75% of the cost of the work done.

There are three grants relevant to owner-occupiers: intermediate grants, improvement grants and repair grants. With all three there will be certain conditions attached by the council.[2]

Intermediate grants are given to pay towards the cost of installing missing standard amenities, which are defined as a fixed bath or shower, hand wash basin, kitchen sink, hot and cold water supply to each, and an inside wc. If you lack any of these you should be able to get a grant. Intermediate grants must be paid by the local council if you qualify. The grant pays a maximum amount for the installation of each of these standard amenities, but can also pay a further amount towards other repairs in order to bring the house up to standard. A disabled person can get a grant towards putting in a second bathroom or wc if the original bathroom or wc is inaccessible because of the disability.

Improvement grants are discretionary and are intended to improve older houses to a good standard – they are not normally available to enlarge a house by adding an extra room. Improvement grants are also available for converting a property into flats. The conditions in respect of the use or state of the property after the improvements have been made will be stricter than with an intermediate grant; you may have to repay some of the grant if you resell within a certain period. Improvement grants are normally only available for homes with a rateable value of under £400 in Greater London, under £225 elsewhere in England and Wales. In Scotland each local authority area has its own limit. Disabled people can also get improvement grants to adapt their home to their needs.

Repair grants are only available on houses or flats built before 1919 and only apply to structural repairs (e.g. roofs, walls, floors or foundations). They are also discretionary.

Listed building grants

If you live in an old building which has been 'listed' as an historic building, you may be able to get a grant to make repairs, and even to carry out maintenance in exceptional circumstances. There are central government and local authority grants for historic buildings.

Government grants for repairs are available for buildings of outstanding historic or architectural interest; the grant can be up to 50% of the cost with no upper limit on the amount. There are also conservation grants for the restoration of buildings which are in outstanding conversation areas, but do not themselves count as outstanding. These grants are administered by the Historic Buildings Council.[3] Similar grants for use in 'non-outstanding' conservation areas are administered by the Civic Trust, which publishes leaflets describing grants in both types of conservation area.[4]

Local authority grants to improve or restore 'historic' buildings vary widely. Loans may also be available from either government or local authorities to pay part of the balance of the cost.

Does your local council approve?

Before you set about extending or enlarging your home, you should check whether you require planning permission. Small extensions which increase the size of the house by less than 10% or are less than 1,750 cubic feet, do not, provided that the house has not already been extended by that much since it was built (or since 1948 if the house was built before then). Houses in conservation areas will probably need planning permission in any case and so will a proposed alteration to a listed building, wherever it may be. If you are in doubt, the best way to find out is to call or write to your local council's planning department. Free leaflets are available from them.[5]

There is also a separate procedure for approval under the Building Regulations for England and Wales. For larger works there is a scale of charges for this approval. There are different regulations for the Inner London Boroughs. Similar laws apply in Scotland and Northern Ireland.

Architects, builders and contractors

The word architect has a specific meaning. It refers to someone qualified as an architect and registered by the Architects Registration Council of the UK. Only people registered by the council may call themselves architects. If someone calls himself an 'architectural consultant' or an 'architectural surveyor', he is unlikely to be registered and may have no qualifications or experience.

Most architects also belong to the Royal Institute of British

Architects and Scottish architects belong too to the Royal Incorporation of Architects in Scotland. RIBA operates a centralised service matching prospective clients to architects interested in the type and size of work proposed.

When commissioning an architect, the same rules about asking about cost apply as when you are dealing with a new solicitor or surveyor (see Chapters 2 and 7).

Finding a good builder for an extension can sometimes be a problem. Recommendation is again the most likely route to success. Otherwise you should provide written specifications for all but the most minor job, and get a written contract confirming the terms under which the builder is supplying his services and about the quality of materials used. The advice of an experienced architect can be invaluable in this respect.

It may not necessarily be a good idea to go to a builder recommended by the architect. Should you fall out with the builder it may be that the architect will consider his other dealings with the builder as well as your interests – and he may not therefore get as much out of the builder as you require.

If you are offered a standard contract by an architect or builder, it could be worth while getting a solicitor to vet it for you. He may be more persuasive than you in getting unreasonable clauses altered, although a solicitor would of course add to the cost so get an estimate from him too before commissioning him.

Another organisation you might approach when considering building work is the Federation of Master Builders at one of their regional offices in Birmingham, Bristol, Cambridge, Cardiff, Leeds, London, Newcastle, Sevenoaks or Southport; in Scotland there is the Scottish Federation of Building Trades Employees in Glasgow.[7] Telephone numbers and addresses can be obtained from the telephone directory or directory enquiries.

For technical information on repairs and the best way to carry out certain building operations, you should contact the Building Research Advisory Service which publishes a number of very useful leaflets.[6] The National Register of Warranted Builders administers a two-year warranty for extensions and other building work. It provides for another builder to come and put things right if the original contractor goes bust or refuses. Member builders subscribe to a code of practice.[7]

VAT and home improvements

Home improvements are no longer zero rated for VAT. That means you have to pay VAT on the bill whoever does the installation. The only situation where a private individual who is not registered for VAT can reclaim the VAT on building materials is if he or she builds a house from scratch. But this only applies if it really is from scratch; if it is joined to any existing building, even a ruin, the VAT refund will not be granted. There is a free leaflet.[8]

Holiday homes

There are two ways you can use a home for holidays. You can buy a second one as a holiday home or you can exchange homes with someone else for your holiday.

Second homes

If you live in town you can have a cottage in the country; the better off often have cottages and flats abroad in Spain, France and Greece. Sometimes a second home is intended as a retirement home and is bought only a short time before retirement, with the intention of selling up the first home upon retirement.

Should you be offered a home with your job – and you already have a home of your own – you could trade in the one you own for a country cottage. This gives you security: should you lose your job you will not have lost out on account of the rise in house prices, and meanwhile you will have had the use of it at weekends.

Buying a home abroad is similar to buying one in the UK. But an added problem is the need to carry out the transaction in a foreign language and also the distance from home which may make maintenance more difficult to organise. For many years, by law you had to pay the investment currency or dollar premium in order to buy property abroad. This used to work out as adding an extra 30% to 50% to the price. However, this was abolished in 1979, and there are now no restrictions on buying property abroad.

Exchanging your home

A more down to earth way of utilising your home for holidays is to arrange to swap it for the duration of your holiday. You go and stay in someone else's home and they come and stay in yours. This can be done within the UK or abroad, and can give you the opportunity of budget holidays in places like America or Australia, which you might not otherwise have been able to visit. There are a couple of directories in which you can advertise for a small charge, and which contain advertisements from people in other countries who want to make exchanges.[9] This can involve you in quite a lot of work in planning and corresponding, but many people who have done it swear by it, and do it year after year.

Falling on hard times

Divorced, widowed or separated

If you become divorced, widowed or separated, you are likely to be short of cash, especially if you have recently moved into your home. If you have young children things may be even worse, because you may not have a job. Whilst you cannot stay in your present house because it is too large and expensive, you cannot afford to buy a smaller one because you may not get a new mortgage.

If you are in this position it is essential to get advice. There are a number of pamphlets which may be of some help, in particular the ones published by SHAC and by the Child Poverty Action Group.[7] These leaflets may also be useful to people who become unemployed or disabled and whose sudden shortage of income turns being a house owner into a very serious problem.

Elderly people

The elderly are another group of homeowners who may have seen better times. By retirement they will generally have paid off the mortgage – and if the main source of income is the state old age pension plus some investments, they will not be eligible for a supplementary pension. In such a case they might consider increasing their income by taking out a Home Income Plan.

The idea is to raise a mortgage which is used to buy an annuity from an insurance company. Sometimes the same insurance company which gives the annuity also grants the mortgage. By a special tax rule the interest on a Home Income Plan loan is eligible for tax relief in the same way as that on a loan to buy a house. So after all the interest and tax relief, and annuity income and tax, the householder gets a net income for life without having to move home. When he or she dies the insurance company is repaid its loan and the rest of the value of the home goes to whoever is chosen in the will of the deceased. Generally speaking you have to be well over the age of seventy for the plan to be worth while; for a couple, the youngest must be over seventy-five. The Abbey National, Halifax and other building societies, Allied Dunbar Provident and Carlyle Life operate Home Income Plans. for more information consult *The Savers and Investors Guide* which is published annually.

Taking in lodgers

If you need to increase your income, and have the space in your home, you may consider taking a lodger or letting out a room. The tenancy you create will not be protected by the Rent Act if you change your mind and decide you want to get rid of your tenant (see Appendix 1).

Students are often a good idea if there is a college or university near where you live. The college will often vouch for the students and they will only want to rent the room during term time, and perhaps part of the Easter and winter vacations.

Tax on the additional income may be payable and you may need the consent of your building society or whoever has provided your mortgage.

Notes

1 See *Extending Your House*, Consumers' Association.
2 See free leaflet *Home Improvement Grants*, Department of Environment, Welsh Office. *Improve Your Home*, Scottish Information Office. *Why Not Improve Your Home?*, Northern Ireland Housing Executive.
3 England, Wales and Scotland each have their own. For addresses see Appendix 3.
4 *Grants and Loans available for Conservation*, Civic Trust. *Conservation Grants for projects in conservation areas other than those accepted as outstanding*, Civic Trust.
5 *Planning Permission*; *Planning Appeals*; Department of Environment and Welsh Office.
6 A list is contained in HMSO Sectional List of Government Publications, *No. 6, 'Building'*.

7 For addresses, see Appendix 3.
8 *VAT: Refund of VAT to 'do-it-yourself' housebuilders*, Public Notice No. 719, HM Customs & Excise.
9 e.g. Home Interchange Ltd.

11

Moving Out

Having lived in your home for some years you may find you need and can afford a larger one. You may even have thought of the next home before you moved in. According to one survey, 60% of first time buyers expect to move within five years.[1] To find a new home you start all over again with the benefit of the experience you obtained from your first purchase. However, one bit of experience you will not have had is trying to sell a house.

Estate agents

Selling a house may be easy or difficult. If it is going to be difficult, you will want to use an estate agent; if it is easy, you might have a crack at it yourself. The main question you should ask yourself is: are estate agents worth the cost?

There are no longer any fixed scales of fees charged by an agent. Another survey shows wide variation in the charges made by estate agents.[2] This survey reported one lady had paid £480 to an estate agent who found a buyer within twenty-four hours; while another was charged £302, but said it was worth while for having so little trouble. Some of the people in the survey found that they had to pay extra for advertising. And the charges in London and parts of the South-East were generally much higher than in the North; not only was the percentage of the price higher, but higher average prices in the South-East also went to boost the estate agent's commission. A bill might range from 1½% to 3% of the price on an average home, plus VAT. In Scotland, Scottish solicitors have a scale of commission when acting as agents, with a maximum of 1½% plus VAT.

The golden rule when dealing with an estate agent is to find out exactly what he will charge beforehand, whether this includes VAT, and whether you have to pay extra for advertising. Get this in writing from him before you commission him.

Another question to consider is whether to give the house to more than one agent. Quite often an agent will suggest you do not employ another agent but give him a 'sole agency', with or without 'sole selling rights'. A sole agency means that you are obliged to pay him the agreed rate of commission during the period of his agency even if you sell the home through someone else. Sole selling rights means that even if you sell the home yourself you still have to pay his commission.

If you decide to let an agent have a sole agency, and it can be argued that he will try harder if he has one, then you should limit the agency to a specified period of time which is agreed at the outset. Four to six weeks is the usual time. If he does not get you an offer at your asking price or at a price below it which you agree to accept by then, you are free to try another agent. You can grant a joint sole agency to two agents if you like, but this might cost you more. Employing more than two agents can be counter-productive.

Although you have granted a sole agency, the agent may in fact subcontract to other agents. If you really wanted just one agent to deal for you, you may feel cheated; normally, however, this is only done when the property proves difficult to sell.

It is always best to confirm your instructions in writing, saying the basis on which you want him to be employed. Do not rely on just signing a printed form offered by the agent which is likely to include clauses to your disadvantage. Also be sure your agreement with the agent means that you only pay commission if the deal goes through. If you agree to pay for an introduction of 'someone ready and willing' to buy your home, you may unwittingly have committed yourself to paying the agent commission even if, for whatever reason, the deal does not go through. So in particular make it quite clear that you will not pay if for *any* reason he is not 'instrumental' in selling the property.

What agents do

Estate agents sell property by sending details through the post to would-be customers who have previously approached them. An agent with a prominent high street position or who has a good reputation locally is likely to have a larger list of potential buyers than a new agent tucked away on the second floor who appeals for sellers in the local newspaper.

They almost always put up a For Sale board on the property. They sometimes put details on a card in their shop window – often with a photograph. And they sometimes advertise in the press – usually locally, sometimes nationally for higher priced property; if they propose to advertise make sure you are not liable for the cost as an extra.

An estate agent is also the person to tell you how much to ask for – and whether to accept a lower offer. Sometimes different agents quote widely different prices. An example quoted in one survey[2] was of a five bedroomed house which one agent priced at £37,500, a second at £42,000 and a third at £44,000 'for a quick sale', otherwise £46,000. The Housing Research Unit found 50% of sellers thought estate agents' valuations were accurate, and 30% thought them inaccurate.

People are sometimes suspicious that an agent will buy up their property cheaply and then resell for a quick profit; such an agent is unlikely to be a member of one of the estate agents' associations.[3] It might be best to go to a member of such an association although the Estate Agents Act 1979 regulates the conduct of estate agents, who are controlled by the Office of Fair Trading. The OFT can ban someone who it considers unfit to practise from engaging in estate agency. There are also provisions for minimum standards of conduct. The OFT provides a free leaflet.[4]

Auctions

If you have an unusual or expensive house to sell, you may well consider auctioning the property. The auctioneer's fees will be higher than an ordinary agent's, but you may get a better price. One problem is that you may find it more difficult to tie up your purchase with your sale.

You can set a reserve price on the minimum you would sell for, and you would be advised to do so. However, if the bidding does not reach your reserve, you will have to pay the auctioneer's fee and will not have sold your house.

Selling your home without an agent

Saving money is the main reason for selling your home without the services of an estate agent, and if you persevere there is a pretty good chance of success. The first thing to do is to find out what price to ask. One way to do this is to ask a couple of estate agents to call and see how much they say they can get for it; another is to look at similar homes nearby, either in estate agents' windows or in local newspapers, and see what is being asked for them.

The easiest do-it-yourself sales are to relatives or people you already know through home or work contacts. So it is always a good idea to spread around to as many acquaintances as possible the fact that you want to sell. I bought my first house this way from a friend whose agents had failed to sell it.

Next you might look in the 'Property Wanted' column of your local newspaper to see if anyone is looking for property in your area. Where these adverts are from agents they will normally expect you to pay them commission, but if the advertiser is a member of the public then all you pay is the cost of a telephone call to the advertiser.

A more likely way is for you to advertise in the local paper yourself. Do not stint yourself on the size of advertisement you take – a larger one will be more eye catching, and will have space to include all the best features of your property. If you have kept the particulars you were given when you bought the property, this might be a basis when you have not a clue where to start. The best way to count the cost of advertising is to compare your total so far with what you would have paid in agents' fees. If an agent quoted you £800 and each advertisement costs £80, remember you have nine to go if the first does not bring about a sale.

It is worth knowing that the response to your advertisement can be affected by all manner of events entirely unconnected with your property. These include popular sports events on television, good weather (which can stop people reading the newspapers so thoroughly or at all) or bad economic news, higher interest rates and suggested mortgage famines which deter people from moving at all. Do not use a box number and do include telephone numbers attended at all times (home and office) or specify the times if necessary.

You can also make your own For Sale board. This may be worth while as many people tour the district in which they want to buy, looking for For Sale boards – a reason why estate agents always suggest them.

In some areas there are property shops or services which will display details of your home in a shop, send particulars out on a mailing list, or store them in a computer. You should regard these as an alternative to advertising in a newspaper and should try to assess whether they are worth using in relation to cost. Estate agents may well respond to your advertisements, claiming they have a buyer on their books most anxious to purchase your type of property. Remember, you will have to pay their commission if their client buys your home.

Showing people round your home

Whether or not you use an estate agent, it will often be left to you to show prospective buyers round your home. Always show it off to best advantage. Make sure it is not cold in winter or too warm in summer. Always have things as tidy as possible and show off any features which are not immediately obvious – like special controls on the central heating or large fitted cupboards.

Once you have done it a few times, you will develop a patter, pointing out the view from the room with the best view, talking about the convenient situation for shops and public transport and so on. There is no harm in touching up decorations, especially outside, or giving the place a spring-clean beforehand. Having the house redecorated inside shortly before you leave may put off as many people as it encourages; they will assume you have covered up some defect – which you may of course have done.

Furniture removers

Having bought your new home and sold your old one, the remaining thing left to do is to arrange to move your furniture from your old to your new home.

As with all the other services described in this book, the same advice applies: get a quote, preferably written, in advance. You can find the name of removal firms in local newspapers, in the Yellow Pages of the telephone directory or by recommendation. Ask two or three to come round: they will want to take a note of what you have, and where you are moving to, in order to work out how much they will charge. There can be large variations in the estimates you receive. In May 1988 *Which?* reported quotes of £396 to £543 for a 262 mile move, and quotes of £317 to £597 for a two mile move.

When removal firms pack all your china for you, they usually undertake to replace anything they break, or compensate you if they cannot. They may be as cheap as hiring a van and trying to do it yourself. Some removers ask to be paid in advance: it would be best to retain payment until the move has been completed to your satisfaction.

If you have a small amount to move and are moving a long distance you might end up paying less if you have your belongings moved as a part load. As with so much else, firms recommended by satisfied customers whom you know are likely to be best.

Before you move out

With the day of your move planned, there are just a few remaining things to be done:

1 Notify the gas, electricity and telephone companies of the date you are moving out and the name of the new owner. Tell them your new address so they can send you a refund of any standing charge paid in advance. The gas and electricity companies will want to come and read the meters, to calculate your final account. If you have a water meter that meter will have to be read too.
2 Cancel the milk and newspapers and pay the bills. If you are leaving the area, pay your bills at any local shops before you leave.
3 Draw up a circular letter informing everyone of your new address and telephone number, and get it photocopied. Send it to

your bank, insurance companies, National Savings (you wouldn't want your Premium Bond winnings to go astray, would you?), building society accounts, stock and share holdings, club memberships, HP companies and driving licence and car tax centres. Include the reference number for each company on the circular letter so they find it easy to trace you.

4 Notify your home contents insurers of the move, and raise the insurance cover if you are moving to a bigger home (with more furniture, carpets, etc.). If you do not have a mortgage, transfer the building's insurance; if you do, the lender will arrange it.

5 Just in case you forget someone, and also so long-lost friends have a chance to look you up, arrange for the Post Office to redirect your letters. There is a charge which varies, depending on how long you want to keep it going. The Post Office needs seven days' notice. Ask for Form P944 Request for Redirection of Mail.

6 If you are moving to a home which is in the same telephone exchange area, you can have your old number transferred to your new home; there is a charge. If not, for up to a year in some areas you can have calls made to the old number intercepted by the exchange, which then tells the caller your new number. There is a connection charge *and* a quarterly charge for this service.

Notes

1 Purchasing Opinions of House Buyers. Housing Research Unit, University of Surrey/Alliance Building Society.
2 *Daily Mail*, 1 February 1978.
3 National Association of Estate Agents; Royal Institution of Chartered Surveyors; Incorporated Society of Valuers and Auctioneers.
4 *Estate Agency: A guide to the Estate Agents Act 1979*, Office of Fair Trading.

12

Your Home and Tax

An owner-occupier is particularly well treated by the taxman. The tax rules you need to know about are summarised in this chapter. Details change annually and are usually announced in the Spring Budget. For more details you should refer to one of the many tax guides available which have new editions every year.[1] This chapter includes details of the 1988 Finance Act.

Tax relief on mortgage interest

Mortgage interest is one of the few things nowadays which the taxman allows you to set against your tax bill, and for most people it is completely straightforward. For every £1 of mortgage interest you pay, you do not have to pay tax on £1 of your income. So if your mortgage interest is £500 a year, you can add another £500 to your tax free allowances.

You are allowed tax relief at the highest rate you pay. If you pay tax at 25%, each £1 of mortgage interest actually costs you 75p after tax relief, i.e. £1 – 25p = 75p. But if you pay 40% tax, you are let off 40p on each £1 of mortgage interest.

Basic rate tax relief is usually given at source, under the MIRAS (Mortgage Interest Relief At Source) scheme; higher rate tax relief has to be claimed later (see p. 117).

You should not have any trouble getting tax relief for buying your own home provided it is your only, or main, one. By main, the taxman normally means a home where you live more than anywhere else. You can also get tax relief on a home you are buying as a retirement home if you live in tied accommodation.

However, you only get full tax relief if the loan is £30,000 or less. If it is more, tax relief is available on the interest paid on the first £30,000 of the loan. The £30,000 limit applies to the 1988–9 tax year but is unlikely to rise in the future.

Up to 1 August 1988, single people with a joint mortgage could each get tax relief on up to £30,000 on their part of the mortgage. This no longer applies and the £30,000 limit relates to the property, not to each person buying it. Mortgages taken out on properties where contracts were exchanged before 1 August 1988 can continue to get tax relief on a mortgage of up to £30,000 per person.

If there is a delay before you move in, you get tax relief for the first twelve months – and this period can be extended if there is a good reason. You can also get tax relief if you rent your house out – if you go away for an overseas job, for example. If for some reason you pay cash, you can take a mortgage within a reasonable time (three months) and still get tax relief.

You can no longer get tax relief on an extra loan for permanent home improvement unless the loan was taken out before 6 April 1988, and provided both old and new loans total £30,000 or less.

Incidentally, if you end up in a houseboat or large caravan as your home you can usually get tax relief on your loan to purchase it.

For more details see one of the tax guides or ask for the booklet available free of charge from any Tax Inspector's office.[2]

How to get tax relief

Tax relief is normally granted at the basic rate at source. This means that for each £100 of interest due, the lender deducts the basic rate of tax. So, when the basic rate is 25%, you pay £100 – £25 = £75.

A few mortgages do not operate in this way. If they do not, basic rate tax relief is not given at source, and you must get all the tax relief from the Inland Revenue. If you are employed, there should be an adjustment on your PAYE Notice of Coding. If you are self-employed, the tax relief should be given in your tax assessment. Tax relief at source means your mortgage payments are lower; otherwise your tax bill is lower.

If you are liable to the 40% higher rate of tax, then you must get this extra tax relief direct from the Inland Revenue. This will be done by an adjustment to your Notice of Coding if you are an employee, or in your tax assessment if you are self-employed.

Capital gains tax

Capital gains tax is a tax which applies to the profit you make when you dispose of an asset for more than you paid for it.

Generally speaking, owner-occupied homes are exempt from capital gains tax. So is one other home you own where a dependent relative lives rent free provided the home was bought for the relative before 6 April 1988.

If for any reason you are away from your home for up to three years, but live in the home both before and after, you do not pay capital gains tax even when you rent it out, provided you return to your home before you sell it, or your then employer requires you under the terms of your employment to work elsewhere.

You can be away for a further four years provided your employer required you to live somewhere else. In this case you do not have to move back afterwards.

If you go to work abroad you can be away for an unlimited time and you need not return to the home before selling, provided your terms of employment required you to work abroad, or when you come to sell they require you to live elsewhere (in the UK or abroad).

If you have two homes, you can choose which is to be your main residence for capital gains tax purposes. This should be done by writing to your tax office within two years of obtaining the second one. If you are required by your employer to live in rented accommodation, nominate the home you own as your main one. Provided you have lived in it for a short while before selling, it will then be free of capital gains tax for up to nine years even if you rent it out – nine not seven years because there is no capital gains tax on the last two years you own a house which has been your main residence. If you want to change your choice, you can backdate your new choice by up to two years. Also, you do not have to worry if you end up with two homes because the sale of your old home falls through. There is no capital gains tax as long as you do not keep both for more than two years.

If you take in lodgers who share accommodation and meals you will not have to pay any capital gains tax on account of them. But if you rent out part of your dwelling separately, you may have to pay capital gains tax on part of the gain when you sell. However, the first £20,000 of such gains, up to and in addition to the amount of the gain on the portion you occupy yourself, is also tax free.

If any part of your home is used exclusively for running a business (you may have indicated this by claiming a proportion of the rates as a business expense) then you may be asked to pay capital gains tax on a proportion of the gain. This is relatively easily avoided. You claim 'roll over' relief on a business asset (e.g. the part of your home you use exclusively as an office) and spend all the proceeds on a similar 'office' in your new home. So long as you keep the business going until you die, or retire at sixty or go abroad and sell after you have left, there is no capital gains tax to pay. This is because there is no capital gains tax on a disposal on death, there are special exemptions on disposal of a business on retirement, and someone resident abroad is not liable to capital gains tax.

Another way round this is to persuade the taxman that you do not use any part of your home exclusively for business use. He may accept this but might not then allow your claim for expenses of maintaining the home which need to be wholly and exclusively incurred for the business to be set against your tax bill.

Extra large gardens – over one acre in size – can incur capital gains tax on the extra size over an acre. And if you are thinking of selling part of your garden, even if it is less than one acre, sell it before you sell the house, and there will be no tax. If you sell it afterwards you are liable to capital gains tax on that transaction.

I am not telling you how to work out capital gains tax because with an owner-occupied home, you should be able to avoid paying it in ninety-nine out of a hundred cases. For more details of this tax, consult a tax guide or get the free Inland Revenue booklets.[3]

Inheritance tax

Inheritance tax is a tax on your estate when you die. It does not trouble most people as there is no tax on money left to a husband or wife on death.

The first £110,000 of money left to anyone else is tax free. The rest is taxed at 40%. The tax applies to gifts made within seven years of death too – although there are reductions if between three and seven years. However you can give away £3,000 in every tax year (which runs from 6 April to 5 April). If you forgot last year you can give £6,000 this year. You can also give £250 to any number of different people provided they have not received gifts under the other exemptions.

This may seem rather irrelevant – you are probably thinking you need a mortgage and cannot afford to give money away. However, someone might like to make a gift to you.

A particularly opportune moment is the occasion of a wedding. Here extra gifts can be made free of inheritance tax. Parents can give up to £5,000 each. Grandparents and great-grandparents can give up to £2,500 each. And anyone else can give up to £1,000. These gifts must be made (or promised in writing) before the wedding, so if your parents have offered to help out with the deposit, get it at the time of your wedding and this could save tax later on.

Notes

1 For example: *Which?* Tax Saving Guide, Consumers' Association; *Allied Dunbar Tax Guide*.
2 IR11, *Tax Treatment of Interest Paid*, Inland Revenue.
3 CGT8, *Capital Gains Tax*; CGT4 *Owner Occupied Houses*, Inland Revenue.

13

How to Cut Costs: A Checklist

Here is a summary of the money-saving hints included elsewhere in this book; for easy cross-reference use the Index.

1 *Renting from the council:* see if they will sell your home to you at a discount; they can also give you a mortgage.
2 *Renting from a private landlord:* if your home is protected by the Rent Act, see whether your landlord will sell it to you at a discount.
3 *Getting married:* money given as a wedding gift can save inheritance tax and can be used to make a deposit on a home.
4 *If you cannot afford the deposit:* ask for a 100% mortgage; try a co-ownership housing association as an alternative to renting; see if you can get into a half rent/half buy scheme run by local authorities or housing associations.
5 *If your deposit is not large enough:* see whether a bank, insurance company or relative will lend you the extra.
6 *If you have a home with your job:* buy a second one of your own now whilst you can afford it and before prices rise.
7 *When offering to buy a house or flat:* do not be afraid to bargain and try to haggle the price down – 5% to 10% off is a reasonable figure; make sure extras are included in the price.
8 *When buying a newly built house:* make sure you have the NHBC inflation-linked warranty.
9 *If the sort of home you want seems too expensive:* try a cheaper area.
10 *Ask for estimates from everyone beforehand:* and get more than one from solicitors, surveyors, removers, estate agents,

architects, builders, decorators, glaziers, plumbers, electricians or anyone else who does work for you. Find out whether VAT is included.

11 *Do not be put off easily when looking for a mortgage:* be ready to move your savings from one building society to another, or your bank account to another bank; do not accept vague refusals; use contacts who can get you a mortgage in place of those who cannot.

12 *Be careful with endowment mortgages:* if you must have one, make sure the insurance policy is the lower cost with-profits type, with a good value insurance company, and with low premiums. A varying payments (gross profile) repayment mortgage is the cheapest method, but not all lenders offer it.

13 *First time buyers:* sign up with the Government Homeloan scheme – it costs you nothing and could qualify you for a small extra loan and a grant in two years' time. If you qualify and cannot wait two years, see if you can be accepted under the 'Late Entry' Application.

14 *When considering becoming self-employed:* move home first; mortgages are difficult to come by for people who have just started up in business or who are not very successful.

15 *Surveys:* ask if the building society valuer will do a structural survey as well for an inclusive fee; if you have a low loan in relation to the price of the home, ask for a reduced valuation fee. If you have the chance to find your own surveyor, find one who specialises in surveys (a building surveyor) rather than one who also acts as an estate agent.

16 *Stamp duty:* make sure that what you pay for the home and what you pay for other things, like carpets, is specified separately if their total value is near the level at which stamp duty applies.

17 *Conveyancing:* ensure that your solicitor can also act for the lender at an inclusive fee. If afterwards the fees are higher than the estimate, ask the solicitor to get a Remuneration Certificate from the Law Society (England and Wales only).

18 *House insurance:* if your house is unusual (e.g. thatched) make sure the building society has done its homework and the insurance company it has chosen is not overcharging. Check by getting your own quotes.

19 *Contents insurance:* a new-for-old policy will save you disappointment if you make a claim. If you live in London or a large city, check whether you can get better cover more cheaply from another company.

20 *Home improvements:* if your house is in a bad state, see whether you can get help from the local council.

21 *Rates or community charge:* pay by monthly instalment and see if you qualify for a rebate.

22 *Disputes:* are best resolved amicably. But if this does not work you would be in a better position with legal expenses insurance to cover your legal costs. Take it out before you get into dispute.

23 *If you fall on hard times:* convert an endowment mortgage to a repayment one, ask if you can extend the repayment term or pay interest only; consider taking in a lodger.

24 *Selling:* have a go at doing it yourself without an estate agent. Make sure you do not sell for too little.

25 *Ending a mortgage:* if there is an alternative to a redemption charge by giving notice, do not forget to give it.

26 *Bridging loans:* make sure your bank does not charge an excessive fee as well as interest. Also make sure a special loan account is opened so that you can claim tax relief.

Appendix 1

Alternatives to Buying

Owning one's home outright is not always an immediate possibility. Here is a summary of the alternatives.

Renting from a council

Council rents tend to reflect the age, position and locality of a home. The main advantage of a council tenancy is that the rent can be low, the council sees to repairs (although this is often quite slow) and there are no extras to pay. Tenants of modest means are entitled to a rent rebate. One problem in the past has been the lack of mobility of council tenants. The Government has set up two computerised registers of tenants who want to move: the Tenants Exchange Scheme and the National Mobility Scheme. Forms to register a request for a swap, and a leaflet,[1] can be obtained from local councils, new town development corporations, citizens' advice bureaux or housing advice centres. Under the Tenants Charter contained in the Housing Act 1980, council tenants have the right to take in lodgers and sublet part of their home; can improve the home and do outside decorations; and have to be consulted and be given information about matters concerning them.

They also have security of tenure except for a limited number of excluded categories (see list on p. 32). This means that a member of the tenant's family living with him or her for six months or more before his or her death has the right to succeed to the tenancy, whatever the tenancy agreement says.

However, there are grounds for eviction even for secure tenants. These include persistent non-payment of rent, nuisance to neighbours, use of the home for illegal purposes, damage or neglect of the home or common parts, or material misrepresentation by the tenant in his application for the tenancy. And in certain circumstances the tenant may be moved to 'suitable alternative accommodation', for example where the council wishes to demolish or rebuild the home, or where the housing was provided for a special purpose, as for the disabled.

Security of tenure brings another important advantage and that is the right to buy your home. For more details see Chapter 3.

Council homes are usually allocated by people getting their names on a waiting list and most lists use a system of points – you get more points if you have young children, are ill or disabled, live in overcrowded or unsanitary conditions and so on. These waiting lists are not always as long as they have been in the past but you must usually continue to live within the council's boundaries to qualify. You can sometimes jump the queue if you are regarded as a 'key' worker – often these are public employees such as district nurses. And if you are prepared to live in older, less attractive accommodation, you might find a home, at least temporarily.

New town development corporations

New town development corporations were set up to organise new towns. Once the town is well established a local council is formed and the housing is passed to the local authority. Tenancies in new towns are very similar to council tenancies although they may be more attractive places to live in and have a less 'municipal' look about them. They may also be easier to obtain than council tenancies because by definition new towns need to attract a new population and they must provide housing, otherwise no one will come. Tenants have the same rights as council tenants.

Housing associations

Ordinary housing associations

Housing associations are non-profit making bodies run by voluntary committees of at least seven people. The Tenants Charter applies to most housing association tenancies as it does to council tenancies.

The right to buy applies to the tenancies of most non-charitable housing associations.

Rents of housing association tenancies can be set by the Rent Officer in the same way as rents for regulated tenants (see p. 129). Housing associations nowadays get a lot of money for new development from local councils and in return the council nominates as many as 50% of the prospective new tenants. In practice they are rather like council tenancies. An official leaflet is available.[2]

Housing associations are often local and vary in size from those with just a few homes to some with several hundred. But they account for about 1% of the total number of homes in the UK. The Housing Corporation keeps a register of several thousand associations and lends money to them. The National Federation of Housing Associations publishes a directory of housing associations in London.

Co-ownership housing societies

To begin with, groups of architects, solicitors, builders, estate agents and so on with the necessary technical expertise get together to plan a scheme. They may not intend to live there – but form the planning committee rather like in an ordinary housing association.

The difference comes about when the co-owners move in. Each pays a nominal fee to become a member of the society and then pays rent based on his share of the mortgage payments which the society is paying. These payments are often called rent and each member has a tenancy agreement outlining his obligations. After the first twelve months, if he keeps his part of the bargain, he cannot be evicted.

When a member leaves, arrangements vary. But a typical scheme might return to him what he has contributed to paying off the capital on the mortgage (provided he stays for five years or more) plus a proportion of the rise in the 'co-ownership' value of the property. The co-ownership value is not the same as the market value and depends on how much the new tenant is being asked to pay in rent. People have been disappointed at what they got when they moved.

The sort of people who might find co-ownership worth considering are people retiring or who do not already own their own home and are too old to get a mortgage – they may want a better standard than their private renting, or previously had a home with a job. If you do not qualify for a council house or flat and do not like the idea of being responsible for maintenance, then co-ownership is a solution.

The disadvantage is that you may find it difficult finding a vacancy, as so few are in existence. The Housing Corporation has information on existing co-ownership societies. It also helps people to organise their own self-build housing co-operatives.[3]

Home with the job

If you are a publican, vicar, caretaker, farm worker, game keeper, live-in domestic help or you are in the armed forces, police or fire services you are quite likely to get a home with your job. Generally speaking, if you lose your job you lose your home; and if you die your dependents have no right to go on living there. However, farm workers have special protection.[4]

Ex-servicemen who leave the forces after 21 December 1979 who become 'secure' council tenants can have their years in forces accommodation added to the years in council accommodation when calculating the discount under the Right to Buy (see p. 30).

Some employers insist that you live in the tied accommodation so you might not want to consider buying your own home until you need to. Many people who live in such tied accommodation think it is wise to buy their home as soon as they can afford it – even though it may be some time before they will want to occupy it. Meanwhile they can rent it out. There are special provisions in the Rent Act to ensure that you can get the accommodation back when you need it as a retirement home.[5]

Renting from a private landlord

Nowadays, private rented accommodation is usually only readily available at astronomical rents suitable for diplomats or visiting businessmen. Anything else which comes on the market is likely to have queues outside the front door in response to a small classified advertisement.

Rents and the security of tenants have been governed by special laws since 1915. They have changed over the years with the result that some existing or 'sitting' tenants have more rights than a new tenant moving in. The result is that 'sitting' tenants have very little incentive ever to move – because nowhere other than in their existing tenancy are they likely to find such good security at such a low rent. But they often suffer from living in a badly maintained building – with a landlord reluctant to carry out repairs as he cannot get the tenant to contribute.

The rules determining the protection available to different sorts of private tenancies are complicated. Most properties come within the scope of the Rent Act 1977 if their rateable value was less than or equal to £750 (£1,500 in Greater London) on 1 April 1973.[6]

Private tenants of modest means can apply for rent allowances (income support) from their local council to pay towards the cost of the rent provided their savings and investments are less than £8,000.

Regulated tenancies

The regulated tenant, once he is in occupation, has full security of tenure. His landlord can rarely evict him and the rent he is entitled to charge is strictly regulated. Such a tenant is often referred to as a 'sitting tenant' although the phrase 'regulated tenant' is the legal term. A 'statutory' tenancy occurs when the period of the original agreement between landlord and tenant runs out or is terminated by the landlord having given 'notice to quit' on a special form. But the landlord cannot enforce his notice and the tenant can continue to live there. If your landlord lives under the same roof, see also the section on *restricted contracts* below.

If a tenant persistently does not pay the rent, annoys neighbours, sublets the whole home or overcharges a subtenant, a court may give a landlord possession. There is also provision for a landlord to get a court order to move a tenant to 'suitable alternative accommodation' which a sitting tenant might regard as tantamount to eviction.[7]

There are a few grounds where a court *must* grant possession of a statutory tenancy to a landlord. The most important are where the landlord previously lived in the accommodation and wants it back for himself or certain members of his family with whom he lives; or where the landlord bought the home to retire to and let it out before retirement. In either case the landlord must have notified the tenant in writing before he let him move in that he would want it back again for one of these reasons.[7]

Sitting tenants are often in a good position to buy their home at less than the market price. Discounts of 20%, 30% or even 50% have been known. Unfortunately, many tenants do not take the opportunity and sometimes the landlord is unwilling to sell at what the tenant regards as a realistic price. If the home is in reasonably good repair, an offer from a landlord to sell to a sitting tenant should be considered very seriously. The tenant will be in a strong position to knock down the asking price and he should remember that the next time an offer is made, the price may be much higher.

The rent of a regulated tenancy can be fixed by the Rent Officer, a statutory official who can usually be found at your local council offices. On application of a landlord or tenant, he fixes what he regards as the 'fair rent'. He enters it on the Rent Register and it is then known as a registered rent. The rent once registered lasts for two years, after which the landlord can ask for an increase. He can get an increase before this period is up if the rent includes payment for services or rates and the cost of these has gone up. The rent increase is phased; half of the increase in the first year, though rises in the cost of services are charged in full.

Fair rents are often a lot less than the rents charged on the open market. Your attitude to the Rent Officer depends on whether you are a landlord or tenant. If either landlord or tenant disagrees with the Rent Officer, he can appeal to a Rent Assessment Committee.[7] In practice the rents tend to be based on what is being registered on comparable properties in the locality.

New regulated tenancies are now difficult to come by, especially in London. If you have one already it could be well worth enquiring whether your landlord is prepared to sell at a discount – especially if other tenants in a block of flats, say, have already bought.

A statutory tenancy lasts for as long as the tenant occupies the home. Subject to certain conditions the statutory tenancy can pass on to a family member on the tenant's death. This can happen more than once on the death of the person who succeeded the original statutory tenant.

Restricted contracts

These mainly apply if you started renting on or after 14 August 1974 and you would have a regulated tenancy but for the fact that your flat is part of a house with a resident landlord. If you rented furnished accommodation before that date, you also have a restricted tenancy if you had a resident landlord then. The landlord does not need to share accommodation with you – you both might have self-contained flats in a converted house, say. But the building must not be a purpose built block of flats. If you were a regulated tenant before the landlord moved in, you remain one.

Restricted contracts come under the jurisdiction of the Rent Tribunal which can give tenants limited security of tenure for up to six months at a time. For lettings made on or after 28 November 1980 tenants cannot apply to the Rent Tribunal for security. The Rent Tribunal can also fix a 'reasonable' rent. This may be the same as a 'fair' rent for a regulated tenancy but could be higher as scarcity of accommodation does not have to be ignored. The Rent Tribunal has its own register of rents.

The main advantage of a restricted contract is that it is one of the few types of privately rented accommodation likely to be on offer. The disadvantage is that for new lettings there is no security of tenure. Such accommodation is likely to be furnished.[5]

Shorthold tenancies

This is a tenancy where landlords can let at rents for fixed terms of between one year (to be reduced to six months) and five years. The tenant has security for the length of the term but the landlord has the right to regain possession at the end of the term. An existing *regulated* or *restricted* tenancy cannot be converted to a shorthold tenancy.[8]

Assured tenancies

This tenancy applies to newly built property owned by landlords which have obtained prior government approval. Under the 1988 Housing Act, it is proposed that anyone can grant an assured tenancy on any type of property. Under assured tenancies rents are subject to rules laid down in the Landlord and Tenant Act 1954 (which regulates business tenancies) and are agreed between landlord and tenant. The Rent Acts do not apply to assured tenancies. An assured tenant has the right to renew his lease in most cases but has to pay the going market rent.[9]

Unprotected tenancies

If your landlord is a government department the only limit on your rent is the agreement you make with your landlord, as is the case of homes with high rateable values.

The same applies if you rent accommodation for a genuine holiday, are a student and rent through your college or university, if you get meals with your home (worth say 20% of what you pay in rent), and probably if you signed a 'non-exclusive licence' to occupy (i.e. you share). It also applies if you share with someone and are not mentioned in the agreement with the landlord, get the home with your job (but it must be a *condition* of your employment), or in the unlikely event of your rent being less than two-thirds of the rateable value on 23 March 1965. And if the landlord makes his agreement with a company as tenant, whoever lives in the accommodation does not normally have any rights to have the rent reviewed.

There is no security of tenure in such cases other than that specified in the lease or tenancy agreement. In practice, though, an eviction can be delayed, as a Court Order is required for all forms of tenancies even though the Court must grant such an order at the request of the landlord. The advantage of unprotected tenancies is that they may be available. The disadvantage is that they are often at high rents which can be increased without any outside intervention when the lease expires.

The Housing Act 1988 contains proposals to deregulate new private tenancies further. The Act had not come into effect at the time of writing. Under the proposals all new tenancies will be either 'assured' or 'shorthold'.

If your landlord seeks to evict you against your will you should seek advice from a Housing Aid Centre, Law Centre, Citizens' Advice Bureau or a solicitor at the earliest opportunity.

Notes

1 *Wanting to Move*; *The Tenants Charter*; *Right to Repair*, Department of Environment, Welsh Office.
2 *Housing Association Rents*, Department of Environment, Welsh Office.
3 *Co-ownership: what is it and where*, *Shared Ownership*, Housing Corporation.
4 Rent (Agriculture) Act 1976.

5 See *Letting Rooms in Your Home*; *Letting your Home or Retirement Home*, Department of Environment, Welsh Office; *Rooms to Let*, Scottish Information Office.

6 For homes built since then, it is the first rateable value. Homes above these limits may also fall within its scope if the present rateable value is above these limits but a previous rateable value was below former limits. The rules are in the Rent Act, 1977. In Scotland the system is broadly the same but is covered by its own acts. Northern Ireland has a different system of rent control – details can be obtained from the Northern Ireland Housing Executive.

7 See also the leaflets: *Regulated Tenancies*; *Notice to Quit*; Department of Environment, Welsh Office, Scottish Information Office.

8 See the leaflets: *Shorthold Tenancies*, Department of Environment, Welsh Office; *Short Tenancies*, Scottish Information Office.

9 For more details see the leaflet *Assured Tenancies*, Department of Environment, Welsh Office.

Appendix 2

Mortgage Repayment Tables

These tables show the monthly payments you would make to a building society at different rates of interest and over different periods of time. They can be used whether the building society operates tax relief at source or not.

Where tax relief at source applies, the interest rate to use is the quoted rate less the current basic tax rate. For instance, where the quoted mortgage rate is 10%, and the basic rate of tax is 25%, you look up 7½% in the tables. Other common rates, with the rate after 25% tax relief in brackets, are: 9% (6.75%), 9½% (7.125%), 9.8% (7.35%), 10½% (7.875%), 11% (8.25%), 11¼% (8.4375%), 11¾% (8.8125%), 12¼% (9.1875%).

The tables do not apply to mortgages which have varying payments, which most banks and some building societies operate. In that case the payment is different each year, and sometimes each month with some of the banks.

Neither do these tables apply to endowment mortgages where you pay interest only, and an insurance premium separately.

To find out the payments on your mortgage, multiply the figure for your rate of interest and mortgage term by the number of thousands of pounds of your mortgage. For example if you have borrowed £30,000 at an interest rate (after 25% tax relief) of 7½%, over twenty-five years, multiply the figure in the table for a loan of £1,000 by 30. So £7.48 × 30 = £224.40.

I am grateful to the Nationwide Anglia Building Society for supplying most of the figures.

Monthly repayments of capital and interest on each £1,000 of a loan.

Rate	TERM OF YEARS *10*	*15*	*20*	*25*	*30*	*35*
%	*£*	*£*	*£*	*£*	*£*	*£*
5.0	10.80	8.03	6.69	5.92	5.43	5.09
5.1	10.85	8.09	6.75	5.98	5.49	5.16
5.2	10.90	8.14	6.81	6.04	5.55	5.22
5.25	10.93	8.17	6.83	6.07	5.58	5.26
5.3	10.95	8.20	6.86	6.10	5.61	5.29
5.4	11.01	8.25	6.92	6.16	5.68	5.35
5.5	11.06	8.31	6.92	6.22	5.74	5.42
5.6	11.11	8.36	7.04	6.28	5.80	5.49
5.7	11.17	8.42	7.09	6.34	5.87	5.55
5.75	11.19	8.45	7.12	6.37	5.90	5.59
5.8	11.22	8.47	7.15	6.40	5.93	5.62
5.9	11.27	8.53	7.21	6.46	5.99	5.59
6.0	11.33	8.59	7.27	6.52	6.06	5.75
6.1	11.38	8.64	7.33	6.59	6.12	5.82
6.2	11.43	8.70	7.39	6.65	6.19	5.89
6.25	11.46	8.73	7.42	6.68	6.22	5.92
6.3	11.49	8.75	7.45	6.71	6.25	5.96
6.4	11.54	8.81	7.51	6.77	6.32	6.02
6.5	11.60	8.87	7.57	6.84	6.39	6.09
6.6	11.65	8.92	7.63	6.90	6.45	6.16
6.7	11.71	8.98	7.69	6.96	6.52	6.23
6.75	11.73	9.01	7.72	7.00	6.55	6.27
6.8	11.76	9.04	7.75	7.03	6.59	6.30
6.9	11.82	9.10	7.81	7.09	6.65	6.37
7.0	11.87	9.15	7.87	7.16	6.72	6.44
7.1	11.92	9.21	7.93	7.22	6.79	6.51
7.2	11.98	9.27	7.99	7.29	6.86	6.58
7.25	12.01	9.30	8.02	7.32	6.89	6.62
7.35	12.06	9.35	8.08	7.38	6.95	6.68
7.4	12.09	9.39	8.12	7.42	6.99	6.72
7.5	12.15	9.45	8.18	7.48	7.06	6.80
7.6	12.20	9.50	8.24	7.55	7.13	6.87
7.7	12.26	9.56	8.30	7.61	7.20	6.94
7.75	12.28	9.59	8.34	7.65	7.23	6.97
7.875	12.35	9.66	8.41	7.72	7.32	7.06
7.9	12.37	9.68	8.43	7.74	7.34	7.08

	TERM OF YEARS					
Rate	*10*	*15*	*20*	*25*	*30*	*35*
%	*£*	*£*	*£*	*£*	*£*	*£*
8.0	12.42	9.74	8.49	7.81	7.41	7.16
8.1	12.48	9.80	8.56	7.88	7.48	7.23
8.225	12.55	9.87	8.63	7.96	7.56	7.31
8.25	12.56	9.89	8.65	7.98	7.58	7.34
8.3	12.59	9.92	8.68	8.01	7.62	7.37
8.4	12.65	9.98	8.75	8.08	7.69	7.45
8.5	12.71	10.04	8.81	8.15	7.76	7.52
8.575	12.74	10.08	8.85	8.19	7.81	7.57
8.7	12.82	10.16	8.94	8.28	7.90	7.67
8.75	12.85	10.19	8.97	8.32	7.94	7.71
8.8125	12.88	10.22	9.01	8.36	7.98	7.75
8.9	12.93	10.28	9.06	8.42	8.04	7.81
9.0	12.99	10.34	9.13	8.49	8.12	7.89
9.1	13.05	10.40	9.20	8.56	8.19	7.97
9.2	13.10	10.47	9.26	8.63	8.26	8.04
9.275	13.14	10.51	9.31	8.67	8.31	8.09
9.3	13.16	10.53	9.33	8.70	8.33	8.12
9.4	13.22	10.59	9.40	8.77	8.41	8.19
9.5	13.28	10.65	9.46	8.83	8.48	8.27
9.625	13.34	10.72	9.54	8.92	8.56	8.36
9.7	13.39	10.77	9.59	8.97	8.62	8.42
9.75	13.42	10.81	9.63	9.01	8.66	8.46
9.8	13.45	10.84	9.66	9.04	8.70	8.49
9.9	13.51	10.90	9.73	9.12	8.77	8.57
10.0	13.57	10.96	9.79	9.19	8.84	8.65
10.15	13.65	11.05	9.89	9.29	8.95	8.76
10.2	13.68	11.09	9.93	9.33	8.99	8.80
10.25	13.71	11.12	9.96	9.36	9.03	8.84
10.3	13.74	11.15	9.99	9.40	9.07	8.88
10.4	13.80	11.21	10.06	9.47	9.14	8.95
10.5	13.86	11.28	10.13	9.54	9.22	9.03
10.6	13.92	11.34	10.20	9.61	9.29	9.11
10.7	13.98	11.40	10.27	9.68	9.37	9.18
10.75	14.01	11.43	10.30	9.72	9.40	9.22
10.8	14.04	11.47	10.33	9.76	9.44	9.26
10.9	14.10	11.53	10.40	9.83	9.52	9.34

Rate %	TERM OF YEARS *10* £	*15* £	*20* £	*25* £	*30* £	*35* £
11.0	14.16	11.59	10.47	9.90	9.59	9.42
11.1	14.21	11.66	10.54	9.97	9.67	9.49
11.2	14.27	11.72	10.61	10.04	9.74	9.57
11.25	14.30	11.75	10.64	10.08	9.78	9.61
11.3	14.33	11.79	10.68	10.12	9.82	9.65
11.4	14.39	11.85	10.74	10.19	9.89	9.73
11.5	14.45	11.92	10.81	10.26	9.97	9.81
11.6	14.51	11.98	10.88	10.34	10.04	9.88
11.7	14.57	12.04	10.95	10.41	10.12	9.96
11.75	14.60	12.08	10.99	10.45	10.16	10.00
11.8	14.63	12.11	11.02	10.48	10.20	10.04
11.9	14.69	12.18	11.09	10.56	10.27	10.12
12.0	14.75	12.24	11.16	10.63	10.35	10.20
12.1	14.81	12.31	11.23	10.70	10.43	10.28
12.2	14.87	12.37	11.30	10.78	10.50	10.36
12.25	14.90	12.40	11.34	10.81	10.54	10.40
12.3	14.94	12.44	11.37	10.85	10.58	10.43
12.4	15.00	12.50	11.44	10.93	10.66	10.51
12.5	15.06	12.57	11.51	11.00	10.74	10.59
12.6	15.12	12.63	11.58	11.07	10.81	10.67
12.7	15.18	12.70	11.65	11.15	10.89	10.75
12.75	15.21	12.73	11.69	11.19	10.93	10.79
12.8	15.24	12.77	11.73	11.22	10.97	10.83
12.9	15.30	12.83	11.80	11.30	11.04	10.91
13.0	15.36	12.90	11.87	11.37	11.12	10.99
13.1	15.42	12.97	11.94	11.45	11.20	11.07
13.2	15.49	13.03	12.01	11.52	11.28	11.15
13.25	15.52	13.07	12.05	11.56	11.32	11.19
13.3	15.55	13.10	12.08	11.60	11.36	11.23
13.4	15.61	13.17	12.15	11.67	11.43	11.31
13.5	15.67	13.23	12.23	11.75	11.51	11.39
13.6	15.73	13.30	12.30	11.83	11.59	11.47
13.7	15.79	13.37	12.37	11.90	11.67	11.55
13.75	15.83	13.40	12.41	11.94	11.71	11.59
13.8	15.86	13.44	12.44	11.98	11.75	11.63
13.9	15.92	13.50	12.51	12.05	11.83	11.71

	TERM OF YEARS					
Rate	*10*	*15*	*20*	*25*	*30*	*35*
%	£	£	£	£	£	£
14.0	15.98	13.57	12.59	12.13	11.91	11.79
14.1	16.04	13.64	12.66	12.21	11.98	11.87
14.2	16.11	13.71	12.73	12.28	12.06	11.95
14.25	16.14	13.74	12.77	12.32	12.10	11.99
14.3	16.17	13.78	12.81	12.36	12.14	12.03
14.4	16.23	13.84	12.88	12.44	12.22	12.11
14.5	16.29	13.91	12.95	12.51	12.30	12.19
14.6	16.36	13.98	13.02	12.59	12.38	12.28
14.7	16.42	14.05	13.10	12.67	12.46	12.36
14.75	16.45	14.08	13.13	12.70	12.50	12.40
14.8	16.48	14.12	13.17	12.74	12.54	12.44
14.9	16.55	14.19	13.24	12.82	12.62	12.52
15.0	16.61	14.26	13.32	12.90	12.70	12.60
15.1	16.67	14.33	13.39	12.97	12.78	12.68
15.2	16.74	14.39	13.47	13.05	12.86	12.75
15.25	16.77	14.43	13.50	13.09	12.90	12.80
15.3	16.80	14.46	13.54	13.13	12.94	12.84
15.4	16.86	14.56	13.61	13.21	13.02	12.92
15.5	16.93	14.60	13.69	13.28	13.10	13.01
15.6	16.99	14.67	13.76	13.36	13.18	13.09
15.7	17.05	14.74	13.84	13.44	13.26	13.17
15.75	17.09	14.78	13.87	13.48	13.30	13.21
15.8	17.12	14.81	13.91	13.52	13.34	13.25
15.9	17.18	14.88	13.99	15.59	13.42	13.33
16.0	17.25	14.95	14.06	13.67	13.50	13.41
16.1	17.31	15.02	14.13	13.75	13.57	13.49
16.2	17.37	15.09	14.21	13.82	13.65	13.57
16.25	17.40	15.12	14.24	13.86	13.69	13.61
16.3	17.44	15.16	14.28	13.90	13.73	13.65
16.4	17.50	15.23	14.36	13.98	13.81	13.73
16.5	17.56	15.30	14.43	14.06	13.89	13.82
16.6	17.63	15.37	14.51	14.14	13.97	13.90
16.7	17.69	15.44	14.58	14.22	14.05	13.98
16.75	17.73	15.47	14.62	14.26	14.09	14.02
16.8	17.76	15.51	14.66	14.30	14.13	14.06
16.9	17.82	15.58	14.73	14.37	14.22	14.14
17.0	17.89	15.65	14.81	14.45	14.30	14.23

Appendix 3

Useful Addresses

Allied Dunbar Provident
9 Sackville Street, London W1X 1DE. Tel: 01-434 3211.
Issues home income plans whereby elderly people (over 70) can raise an income from their home without moving out.

Architectural Association
34–36 Bedford Square, London WC1B 3ES. Tel: 01-631 1381.
Acts as bookshop and adviser for publications on architecture.

Architects Registration Council of the UK
73 Hallam Street, London W1N 6EE. Tel: 01-580 5861.
Keeps a register of people entitled to call themselves architects. It is their disciplinary body and issues a leaflet containing their code of conduct for architects.

Association of British Insurers
Aldermary House, Queen Street, London EC4N 1TT. Tel: 01-248 4477.
Publishes free leaflets on different types of insurance including one on how to work out rebuilding costs. A forum for complaints against insurance companies.

Blay's Guides
Blay's House, Churchfield Road, Chalfont St Peter, Bucks, SL9 9EW. Tel: 0753-880482.
Publishes Blay's Residential Mortgage Tables updated monthly.

British Association of Removers
277 Gray's Inn Road, London WC1X 8SY. Tel: 01-837 3088.
Will provide details of members in your area. If you are moving abroad, the international section operates an indemnity scheme.

British Chemical Dampcourse Association
16A Witchurch Road, Pangbourne, Reading, RG8 7BP. Tel: 07357-3799.
Has a code of practice and will investigate complaints against members.

British Insurance and Investment Brokers Association
BIIBA House, 14 Bevis Marks, London EC3A 7NT. Tel: 01-623 9043.
Will supply names of local brokers and possibly those who also operate as mortgage brokers.

British Wood Preserving Association
150 Southampton Row, London WC1B 5AL. Tel: 01-837 8217.
Gives advice on preservation of wood against insects, fire and damp. A list of publications is available on request.

Building Centre
26 Store Street, London WC1E 7BT. Tel: 01-637 1022. Enquiry service 0344-884999.
A permanent exhibition of building materials open 9.30–5.15 weekdays; 10–1 Saturdays. It also has a bookshop and manufacturers' catalogues. There are also Building Centres in Bristol, Glasgow and Manchester.

Building Research Advisory Service
Building Research Station, Bucknell Lane, Garston, Watford WD2 7JR. Tel: 0923-674040.
Advises on tricky design and construction problems by telephone, letter or visit, often free of charge. Has some free leaflets and the Building Research Station publishes a series of advisory leaflets which are available through HMSO bookshops.

Building Societies Association

3 Savile Row, London W1X 1AF. Tel: 01-437 0655.
Supplies list of members and free booklet on house purchase called 'Starting Point' with special edition for house purchasers in Scotland.

Burgoyne Alford Insurance

32 North Street, Horsham, Sussex RH12 1RQ. Tel: 0403-211111.
Specialises in thatched and timber buildings.

Castle Books

Westhill Road, Blackdown, Leamington Spa CV32 6RA. Tel: 0926-28370.
Publishes Bradshaw's *Guide to House Buying, Selling and Conveyancing* (£6.95). Bradshaw's *Guide to House Conveyancing for Sitting Tenants* (£3.95). Bradshaw's *DIY Guide to Changing Home Ownership into Joint Names* (or any other gift of property) (£3.95).

Cavity Foam Bureau

PO Box 79, Oldbury, Warley, West Midlands, B69 4PW. Tel: 021-544 4949.
Information about cavity wall insulation.

CGA (Insurance Brokers)

Icknield Way West, Letchworth, Herts, SG6 4AP. Tel: 0462-480011.
Specialise in thatched and timber buildings. Provide address and telephone number of local offices.

Chambers and Newman Insurance Brokers Ltd

Canberra House, 315 Regent Street, London W1R 8AH. Tel: 01-637 4211.
Issues an insurance policy called the Knightel Flat Protection Plan. Underwritten by Cornhill Insurance. This covers long leaseholders who lose occupation of their home through fire, etc. If after two years, they cannot return to their flat, the full market value is paid as a lump sum. In the meantime 10% of the market value is paid each year to provide alternative accommodation.

Child Poverty Action Group
1–5 Bath Street, London EC1V 9PY. Tel: 01-253 3406.
Helpful to people who have fallen on hard times. A price list of publications is available on request.

Consumers' Association
PO Box 44, Hertford SG14 1SH. Tel: 01 486 5544.
Publishers of *Which?*

Conveyancing Fraud
27 Occupation Lane, Woolwich, London SE18 3JQ. Tel: 01-855 2404. This book (£3.95) tells you how to do your own conveyancing. Available through bookshops or directly from author and publisher at the above address. The author also gives three telephone consultations for £5 (particulars in book).

CORGI
St Martin's House, 140 Tottenham Court Road, London W1P 9LN. Tel: 01-387 9185.
This is the Confederation for the Registration of Gas Installers. You can obtain free leaflets explaining what they do and also addresses of regional offices which hold a register of local installers.

Environment, Department of
Publications Distribution, Building 3, Victoria Road, South Ruislip, HA4 0NZ. Tel: 01-845 7788.
Publishes a number of free leaflets on housing which are usually available at Citizens' Advice Bureaux and local council offices; they may also be obtained direct from the above address. In Scotland the Scottish Information Office, in Wales the Welsh Office and in Northern Ireland the Northern Ireland Housing Executive publish similar leaflets.

Federation of Master Builders
33 John Street, London WC1N 2BB. Tel: 01-242 7583.
Will supply names of members in your area. There are regional branches in Birmingham, Bristol, Cambridge, Cardiff, Leeds, Newcastle upon Tyne, Sevenoaks and Southport. Runs the National Register of Warranted Builders.

Federation of Private Residents' Associations
11 Dartmouth Street, London SW1H 9BL. Tel: 01-222 0037.
Gives advice to individual residents and associations in dealing with problems of maintenance, etc. by ground landlords.

FIMBRA
Financial Intermediaries, Managers & Brokers Regulatory Association, Hertsmere House, Marsh Wall, London E14 9RW. Tel: 01-538 8860.
Self-regulatory organisation for independent financial advisers.

Glass and Glazing Federation
44–48 Borough High Street, London SE1 1XB. Tel: 01-403 7177.
Publish a number of free leaflets on glass and double glazing. Will supply names of members in your area, who must abide by their code of ethical practice.

Guarantee Protection Trust Ltd.
PO Box 77, 27 London Road, High Wycombe, Bucks, HP11 1BW. Tel: 0494 447049.
Provides insurance for 'guarantees' by specialist contractors treating woodworm, wet rot, dry rot and rising damp.

Heating and Ventilating Contractors' Association
34 Palace Court, London W2 4JG. Tel: 01-229 2488.
Will supply names of members in your area.

Historic Buildings and Monuments Commission
Fortress House, 23 Savile Row, London W1X 2HE. Tel: 01-734 6010.
Provides information on repair grants. You will also find the Historic Buildings Bureau at the same address; this issues a list of historic buildings for sale, including abandoned railway stations and the like. There are also Historic Buildings Councils for Scotland and Wales in Edinburgh and Cardiff.

HMSO (Her Majesty's Stationery Office)
49 High Holborn, London WC1V 6HB. Enquiries: Tel: 01-211 5656.

The address above is the Government bookshop where you can obtain all government publications (other than free leaflets). A free list of publications 'Sectional list No. 61 Building' is available which can be obtained by callers to the above address or at one of the other government bookshops in Belfast, Birmingham, Bristol, Cardiff, Edinburgh or Manchester. London area mail orders should go to HMSO Publications Centre. PO Box 276, London SW8 5DT.

Home Interchange Ltd.
8 Hillside, Farningham, Kent DA4 0DD. Tel: 0322-864527.
Publishes directory of home exchanges for holidays in UK, North America, Europe, Australasia and elsewhere.

Housing Corporation
149 Tottenham Court Road, London WIP OBN. Tel: 01-387 9466.
Government sponsored organisation responsible for housing associations. There are regional offices in Cardiff, Croydon, Edinburgh, Exeter, Glasgow, Leeds, Leicester, Liverpool, Manchester and Wolverhampton. Publications include information on housing associations and shared ownership. List of publications on request.

Incorporated Association of Architects and Surveyors
Jubilee House, Billing Brook Road, Weston Favell, Northampton NN3 4NW. Tel: 0604-404121.

Incorporated Law Society of Northern Ireland
Law Society House, 90–106 Victoria Street, Belfast BT1 3JZ. Tel: 0232-231614.
The professional body for solicitors in Northern Ireland.

Incorporated Society of Valuers and Auctioneers
3 Cadogan Gate, London SW1X OAS. Tel: 01-235 2282.
Members abide by a code of conduct. Publishes a number of free leaflets including *Buying and Selling at Auction*.

Insurance Ombudsman Bureau
31 Southampton Row, London WC1B 5HJ. Tel: 01-242 8613.
Investigates consumer complaints and arbitrates on claims made against its members.

Land Registry
32 Lincoln's Inn Fields, London WC2A 3PH. Tel: 01-405 3488.
Government body which registers property ownership in England and Wales. Check with the head office which of the district land registries in Birkenhead, Croydon, Durham, Gloucester, Harrow, Lytham St Annes, Nottingham, Peterborough, Plymouth, Stevenage, Swansea, Tunbridge Wells and Weymouth, covers your area. Explanatory leaflets on the work of the Land Registry are available from HMSO.

Law Society
113 Chancery Lane, London WC2A 1PL. Tel: 01-242 1222.
The professional body for solicitors in England and Wales. Has free leaflets explaining why it is best to use a solicitor.

Law Society of Scotland
26 Drumsheugh Gardens, Edinburgh EH3 7YR. Tel: 031-226 7411.
The professional body for solicitors in Scotland. Publishes a free leaflet 'Buying or Selling a House' and will investigate complaints made about Scottish solicitors.

Money Management
FT Business Publishing Ltd., Greystoke Place, Fetter Lane, London EC4A 1ND. Tel: 01-405 6969.
A monthly magazine available on subscription which has regular surveys on insurance, mortgage terms, etc. Single back copies available.

National Association of Conveyancers
44 London Road, Kingston upon Thames, Surrey, KT2 6QF. Tel: 01-549 3636.
Members include low cost conveyancing firms. Members have to abide by certain rules. Will provide list of members.

National Association of Estate Agents
Arbon House, 21 Jury Street, Warwick CV34 4EH. Tel: 0926-496800.
Will supply names of members in your area. Members have to abide by a code of conduct. Runs National Home Link Service with 600

members. Enables you to get details of homes outside your area from an estate agent within your area.

National Cavity Insulation Association
PO Box 12, Haslemere, Surrey GU27 3AN. Tel: 0428-54011.
Members must work to certain minimum standards. Free leaflet and names of members in your area available.

National House Building Council
Chiltern Avenue, Amersham, Bucks HP6 5AP. Tel: 0494-434477 or 01-637 1248 for leaflets.
Maintains standards for newly built houses and blocks of flats including conversions and underwrites aftersales service and warranty. Several free leaflets are available. Scotland and Northern Ireland have offices in Edinburgh and Belfast.

National Inspection Council for Electrical Installation Contracting
Vintage House, 37 Albert Embankment, London SE1 7VJ. Tel: 01-582 7746.
Publishes a list of approved electrical contractors which includes both large and small firms.

National Register of Warranted Builders
A warranty scheme to cover faulty workmanship and materials for up to two years after the job is finished. For address see Federation of Master Builders.

Northern Ireland Housing Executive
2 Adelaide Street, Belfast BT2 8PB. Tel: 0232-240588.
The body responsible for housing in Northern Ireland; a sort of national local authority. Free leaflets available on home improvement grants and other topics.

Office of Fair Trading
Field House, 15–25 Breams Buildings, London EC4A 1PR. Tel: 01-242 2858.
A statutory body which looks after consumer interests. It also administers the Consumer Credit Act and regulates estate agents.

Will deal with or pass on complaints on these and other consumer issues.

Royal Incorporation of Architects in Scotland
15 Rutland Square, Edinburgh EH1 2BE. Tel: 031-229 7205.
Professional body for architects in Scotland.

Royal Institute of British Architects
66 Portland Place, London W1N 4AD. Tel: 01-580 5533.
Provides Clients' Advisory Service to help you find an architect suitable for your particular job. Free leaflets available.

Royal Institution of Chartered Surveyors
12 Great George Street, Parliament Square, London SW1P 3AD. Tel: 01-222 7000.
Members consist of surveyors and building surveyors who may also be estate agents. Free leaflets available.

SHAC (The London Housing Aid Centre)
189A Old Brompton Road, London SW5 OAR. Tel: 01-373 7276.
Gives free advice on housing problems, especially for homeless and less well off. List of publications available.

Solicitors Complaints Bureau
Portland House, Stag Place, London SW1E 5BL. Tel: 01-834 2288.
Handles complaints against solicitors.

Thatchowners (Insurance Agency)
Victoria House, 38 Hampton Road, Twickenham, Middlesex TW2 5QB. Tel: 01-755 0993.
Specialises in thatched and timber buildings.

The Savers and Investors Guide
Wisebuy Publications, 25 West Cottages, London NW6 1RS. Tel: 01-433 1121.
This book (£3.95) gives information on all ways of saving and investing, including Home Income Plans. From bookshops or, plus 50p p&p, from the publishers.

Index